Legal Cannabis Will Be Bigger Than Cryptos

Learn Why You Should Invest Right Now

A Beginner Guide To CBD Investing

By

Ernie Braveboy

Get Your Free Copy of

How to be a Real Estate Millionaire

To Get Your Free Copy, Open the Link

https://ebraveboy_3ee2.gr8.com/

INTRODUCTION

This book will show you how you can invest and profit in the legalized Cannabis industry.

It is no secret that we are all admirers of early cryptocurrency investors. They have attained financial success that most of us can only dream of.

One article in Investopedia showed that if you invested $100 in bitcoin back in 2011, that measly sum would have grown in value to a staggering $2 million dollars in 2018, along with a handsome $53,000 pocket change.

Think about it. If you could afford $1000 back then, you would have easily become very rich just by buying bitcoin and holding it. Unfortunately, that ship has sailed. Today, you wouldn't expect such phenomenal returns from buying and holding bitcoin. The dust has settled.

If you have benefited from this wonderful opportunity, good for you. But this doesn't mean that you should despair if you didn't. Life isn't capricious, similar opportunities are always coming up and it is up to you take advantage of them early enough.

Legal cannabis is one such opportunity.

The main message in this book is that by investing in legal Cannabis right now, you will be properly positioning yourself to take advantage of the next big asset price bubble, and get rich in the process.

Why do I say this?

Well you see, recently, the world has begun expressing interest in Cannabis. People are waking up to the fact that Cannabis may not be that bad after all. Its reputation is turning into something that most people would be happy to be associated with. For one thing - as you will see later on in this book – CBD, which is a compound found in the plant offers an impressive array of health benefits.

Because of this and many other reasons, leading nations have already started legalizing Cannabis. For instance, the U.S has made cannabis legal in over 20 states. There is ample indication that the government could take this decision a notch higher and legalize it nationally.

Canada is another big nation that has also legalized Cannabis. In fact, it has legalized both recreational and medical marijuana, according to a report by the CNN. It is also the second country (after Uruguay) to legalize Cannabis at a national level. As you can imagine, at this rate, it won't be long before other nations follow suit.

Even Wall Street has begun taking note and supporting this new development. Business Insider reports that JP Morgan and Guggenheim are raising venture capital for investing in the upcoming marijuana industry.

One analyst at CNBC describes that the transformation taking place in the Cannabis industry is unlike anything he has ever seen. He estimates that the Cannabis industry could be raking in a reputable $200 billion a year. This is a far cry from the $20 billion a year circulating in the cryptocurrency market.

And that's not all; he goes on to say that this number is likely to double every year for the next 6 to 7 years! This is why I maintain that legal Cannabis will be bigger than Cryptocurrencies.

If you are looking at these numbers and thinking, "Oh man...I must become a part of this..." you are right. This is a wonderful opportunity and there has never been a better time to get in than now. You can't afford to pass it up.

But there is a catch... You may not have the slightest idea of how you can get started and how to go about things. There is a lot of information out there purporting to guide you through this investment abyss. Many ideas abound - some good and some bad.

How do you tell the difference between what you need to trust and what you shouldn't? And do you even have the time to sift through all that endless stream of information? I'm guessing you don't. After all, you have only so many hours per day. And life is short. If there is a chance that you could acquire reliable information in one place at your convenience, you need to take it.

The good news is that this book serves that purpose. In it, you will learn everything you need to know about the Cannabis industry from start to finish and how you can go about investing in it. You will receive step by step guidance on how you can go about complicated procedures like selecting the right CBD stock, planting a Cannabis plant and so on.

What's more; I will be explaining all these things in language that is easy to understand. It will be as if I am right there guiding you by the hand on what you need to do.

By the time you are done reading this book, you will no longer have lingering reservations in your mind on what the right call is. You will be ready to get up and make your investment right away with confidence.

Does that sound good enough for you? Good. Then let's get down to business.

Thanks again for purchasing this book. I hope you enjoy it!

© **Copyright 2019 - All rights reserved.**

This document is geared towards providing exact and reliable information in regards to the topic and issue covered. The publication is sold with the idea that the publisher is not required to render accounting, officially permitted, or otherwise, qualified services. If advice is necessary, legal or professional, a practiced individual in the profession should be ordered.

- From a Declaration of Principles which was accepted and approved equally by a Committee of the American Bar Association and a Committee of Publishers and Associations.

In no way is it legal to reproduce, duplicate, or transmit any part of this document in either electronic means or in printed format. Recording of this publication is strictly prohibited and any storage of this document is not allowed unless with written permission from the publisher. All rights reserved.

The information provided herein is stated to be truthful and consistent, in that any liability, in terms of inattention or otherwise, by any usage or abuse of any policies, processes, or directions contained within is the solitary and utter responsibility of the recipient reader. Under no circumstances will any legal responsibility or blame be held against the publisher for any reparation, damages, or monetary loss due to the information herein, either directly or indirectly.

Respective authors own all copyrights not held by the publisher.

The information herein is offered for informational purposes solely, and is universal as so. The presentation of the information is without contract or any type of guarantee assurance.

The trademarks that are used are without any consent, and the publication of the trademark is without permission or backing by the trademark owner. All trademarks and brands within this book are for clarifying purposes only and are the owned by the owners themselves, not affiliated with this document.

TABLE OF CONTENTS

Introduction iii
The Green Rush 1
A Background On Legalized Marijuana 7
    The History 7
    The Tax Act 8
    Prohibition 9
    Legalization 9
    First IPO 10
Hemp And Marijuana 12
    The Difference 13
        Cultivation 14
        Is There A Difference Between CBD Extracted From Both Plants? 15
About CBD And THC 17
    About Cannabinoids 17
    The Chemical Composition Of CBD And THC 17
    The Endocannabinoid System 18
        How THC Reacts With The Endocannabinoid System 19
        How CBD Reacts With The Endocannabinoid System 19
    About THCV 20
Types Of CBD Products 22
    1: Beauty Products 22
    2: Oil-Based Capsules 24

3: CBD Concentrates 26

4: Drinks 28

5: CBD Edibles 29

6: Pet Products 30

7: Suppositories 31

8: Oil-Based CBD Tinctures 32

9: Topicals/ Rubs/ Balms 34

10: Transdermal Patches 35

11: Vape Products 36

12: Water-Soluble CBD Powder 37

How You Can Invest In Cannabis 38

Why Invest In Legal Cannabis? 38

How To Ride The Cannabis Wave: To Make Money In The Cannabis Industry 49

#1. Starting a Cannabis blog 49

#2. Open A Cannabis Dispensary 58

#3. Become And Edibles Chef 70

#4. Run A Cannabis Lab 75

#5. Start An Online Shop 81

#6. Growing Cannabis 90

#7. Buying Stock In Cannabis Companies 107

Conclusion 121

x

Legal Cannabis Will Be Bigger Than Cryptos

THE GREEN RUSH

There is a word for what has been happening in the Cannabis industry lately, and that word is "the green rush."

You remember the gold rush, don't you? A time when there was a huge influx of people looking to cash in on the discovery of gold in California. The same thing could be happening in the legal marijuana industry, as more and more people realize that it could easily become the next big thing.

But how exactly is this happening?

We have already talked about some of it. Let's spend some time looking at it on a much deeper level.

Let's start with the numbers. You may be shocked to find out that the traction on the legal marijuana industry has been so strong, it has even rivaled some mainstream household brands.

One report filed by the statistics giant Statista, which was referenced by the Inc. magazine back in 2015 showed that sales of legal marijuana outdid those of household brands like Dasani, Oreo, Girl Scout cookies and the like, by more than five times.

Think for a minute.

Legal marijuana has been such a powerful force; it has even beaten some of the biggest brands in the world, in organic produce and drinks combined! That is an outstanding record. And so far, there have been no reports of sales slowing down.

As a matter of fact, legal marijuana has done so well, Inc. magazine has even done a report championing it as one of the 8 best industries to launch a business in 2019. And keep in mind that this is happening at a time when marijuana has been legalized only in a number of states. What happens when legalization takes place nationwide or even worldwide? Sales could explode.

Evidence of this happening is everywhere. States that haven't yet pushed for legalization of marijuana are under so much pressure. New York is one state that has faced such an outcry; many residents have even decided to take the matter into their own hands. It is reported that New York residents have been crossing the border over to Massachusetts so that they can buy cannabis products, which have already been legalized in that state.

But that isn't what should shock you the most. The education sector has also been attracted to the craze as well. Florida Gulf Coast University was the first to announce in late 2018 that it was going to offer an undergraduate program on Cannabis Studies. And the response has been encouraging.

Speaking to Wink News, one student taking the program said, "This is my favorite class and I don't want it to end." FGCU director of workforce development told the press that the entire administration is in full support of the program.

Legal Cannabis Will Be Bigger Than Cryptos

The school is aiming at producing a generation of people who will be well equipped to become leaders in the upcoming legal cannabis industry.

This action has inspired other institutions to take the same initiative as well. As at now, top Universities like Harvard, University of Maryland, and Clark University have not been left behind.

This goes on to show you just how far people are willing to go on this matter.

In addition, public perception concerning Cannabis has changed dramatically. Only a little while ago, many people believed that Cannabis was dangerous and should remain banned. Recently, those opinions have changed.

Pew Research Center has been tracking the number of people who support the legalization of Cannabis. There is a staggering difference in the data. Back in 1969, only a mere 12% of people surveyed voted that Cannabis should be made legal. In 1990, that number rose to only 16%.

After 1990, the number of people in support of Cannabis has risen steadily. In 2010, the number became 32%. And at the time of this writing, that number stands at 62%. My guess is, as people become more and more informed, this number is only likely to go up.

But as of the moment, what should matter to you is that more people are in support legalized marijuana than those who don't. And as someone who is considering investing in this industry, this can only be good news for you.

Another evidence of the green rush has been the proliferation of CBD products. Remember, earlier, I stated that CBD is a compound found in the Cannabis plant that has several beneficial uses. Today, we are seeing a number of new different products hitting the marketplace, which contain CBD.

Products range from food, to beauty products, to medicinal products, you name it. The interesting part is; they all come from different vendors. The founder of Populum - one of the leading brands specializing in CBD products – is quoted as saying, "There is apparently even a CBD toothpick".

This is evidence that people have started taking note of the potential of this controversial industry. Otherwise, no one would even go through the trouble of researching, creating and marketing all these products.

That isn't the only development taking place is in this new industry. Societal acceptance has even changed how people consume the products. Today, people no longer have to take the product behind closed doors where nobody would see them and stigmatize them. More and more people are coming out and freely consuming CBD products in public.

This has led to entrepreneurs setting up places that give people the freedom to socialize and still use CBD products. Those places are Cannabis lounges and cafes, and as I write this book, stories about them are trending on the web. For instance, San Francisco boasts having seven such lounges already.

Legal Cannabis Will Be Bigger Than Cryptos

Companies in this new booming industry have risen so fast, such that many of them are already playing in the big leagues, in the stock market. Wall Street professionals who have done their homework on these companies report that some of them have market capitalizations exceeding $1 billion.

Some of these companies include Canopy Growth Corporation, Aurora Cannabis, Aphria, and Cronos Group. Keep in mind that there are several companies in some popular sectors that went public several years ago that haven't yet managed to break through this threshold. The fact that young companies in a relatively new industry have already become so big so quickly is an indication of the power this new form of gold rush is already wielding.

Can you start seeing why and how the green rush could end up being similar to the mania in cryptocurrencies, if not bigger? I hope so.

If you still don't, keep in mind that it is already becoming expensive for some companies to operate in this sector. This is what the CEO of Azuca, Kim Rael is confirming. She says that these days, succeeding in Cannabis has become more difficult. Consolidations and joint efforts are becoming more necessary in order to secure funds, marketing power and other resources.

This can be compared to the sky-high prices that prohibit most people from purchasing enough Bitcoin or Berkshire Hathaway stock today. This is one of the reasons why getting in right now may be your best play, before you are shut off from participating in this lucrative industry.

Now that we are done looking at the green rush, let us now take a closer look into what you will be investing in. After all, you wouldn't want to invest in something that you barely understand, would you? In the coming chapters, we will be looking at everything you need to know about Cannabis down to the paper clips. See you there.

A Background On Legalized Marijuana

Before we dig into the nuts and bolts of Cannabis, we need to first understand the history of how it made its way into our lives. And when it comes to that, Cannabis has had a pretty interesting journey. Read on to find out.

The History

The origins of the Cannabis plant can be traced back to as early as the year 500 B.C. It was predominantly found in Asia. Back then, the plant was mainly used for medicinal purposes only.

The early Asian users discovered that extracts from the plant could be used to treat and control ailments like malaria, inflammation, gout and even depression. They even discovered that it could be used to lower sexual desires.

Afterwards, there was discovery of the psychoactive properties of extracts from the plant. But they put this property to use in ceremonies like religious rituals.

Then, in early 1500s, Spanish people introduced the plant to North America. The colonies back then grew the plant because it was found out that it could produce fiber, which could be used to make ropes and even paper.

In fact, Cannabis was seen as so important then, its growth was even made compulsory. In states like Virginia, Massachusetts and Connecticut, you could even be jailed if you failed to grow the plant. It was even used as way for farmers to pay their taxes. This remained the take on the colonial government for the larger part of the 17th, 18th, and 19th centuries.

Cannabis remained legal in the U.S well into the early 1900s before there was a different turn of events.

It began with the tax act.

The Tax Act

The federal Marijuana tax act was introduced in the year 1937. It was a move by the government to ban the growth and sale of Cannabis by imposing heavy taxes.

It is unclear what brought on this sudden change of heart by the government, but rumors have it that racial association of the plant with Mexicans led to this.

What is clear however, is how serious they considered the matter. Just a day after the law was passed, Samuel Caldwell, a 58-year old farmer was arrested and sentenced to four years of hard labor for the possession of Cannabis.

With this heavy penalty came the disappearance of Cannabis in U.S. The only people who handled it from then on were illegal dealers in the black market.

Public concern over Cannabis was fueled by a film that was released in 1936, which was titled "Reefer Madness". It portrayed Cannabis as highly dangerous and even showed the consequences of its use on the youth of society. It was seen as a gateway to vices like illicit sex and crime.

Prohibition

The government further waged a war on Cannabis by labeling it as a Schedule 1 drug in the Controlled Substances Act of 1970. The president who saw to this was none other than the famous Richard Nixon.

A classification of "Schedule 1" puts Cannabis in the same category as hard drugs such as Heroin, LSD, Ecstasy, Bath Salts and Mescaline. This meant that these drugs were considered very dangerous and highly addictive. They couldn't be used even for health purposes.

This Act effectively sealed the fate of Cannabis, at least for some time.

Legalization

Steps towards legalization of Cannabis began in 1972 after a report named "Marijuana: A signal of Misunderstanding" was filed. The message in the report was that Marijuana wasn't as dangerous as it was labeled to be. It even suggested lesser penalties for small possessions of the drug.

This initiative was however ignored by Nixon's administration.

Legalization, however took its first step in the state of California. The Compassionate Use Act of 1996 allowed the drug to be used in the state for medical purposes only. It was during this time that other states followed suit.

Before the end of the 1900s, four states had legalized the use of Medical Marijuana. Those states were Oregon,

Washington, Alaska, and Maine. The early 2000s saw other states like Nevada, Rhode Island, Hawaii, Vermont, New Mexico and others join the revolution. This date, 33 states have legalized medical marijuana.

But this wasn't all. Recreational marijuana was given consideration as well.

This began with states of Washington and Vermont in 2012. They allowed the use of recreational marijuana for persons over the age of 21. This also allowed businesses to transact the product.

As always, other states joined in. As of this writing, recreational marijuana is legal in up to 11 states in the U.S. The legalizations (including those of Uruguay and Canada) set the stage for the now booming marijuana industry.

However, when marijuana caught the attention of Wall Street, there was no longer any doubt in people's minds that the Cannabis industry was now destined for great things.

First IPO

The most important street in the U.S conducted its first experiment on Cannabis in 2018. This experiment was taking Canadian company, Tilray, public. The IPO surpassed most people's expectations.

The company began trading $23 per share. The price quickly rose to $300. Right now, the company has been valued at over $23 billion.

Legal Cannabis Will Be Bigger Than Cryptos

Today, marijuana has become the talk of the day. Even Google Trends lists "CBD gummies" as the third most searched food term.

Now that you are well equipped with a decent background on Cannabis, let us now delve into the specifics of what it is, and starting with the plant itself.

Hemp and Marijuana

Many people are still new to this legalized Cannabis thing. There are still many lingering questions that have been left unanswered. One of those questions is, "Are hemp and marijuana the same?" I want to spend some time clearing the smoke on this matter.

The short answer to the above question is, "No." But, they are closely related.

First of all, if the two plants were presented in front of you, you wouldn't tell the difference. The two plants look exactly the same. There are no physical characteristics to distinguish the two; the leaves, the flowers and the stem look identical. You wouldn't be able to tell the two apart.

As a matter of fact, both plants belong to the same family. Its name is Cannabaceae. They also belong to the same genus, which is Cannabis. There are three species under this family. They are: Cannabis indica, Cannabis sativa, and Cannabis ruderalis. The surprising thing is that both hemp and marijuana are classified under Cannabis sativa.

So, how did the two ever become different? It turns out; the difference is at a very fundamental level, which I will explain in a bit. But first, let me explain how the name Marijuana came to existence.

The history of Marijuana, along with its name can be traced back to the Mexicans. As I explained in the previous chapter, Cannabis was grown in America, even as early as the 17th Century.

However, the Mexican Revolution, which took place during the period between 1910 and 1920, forced many Mexican people (almost a million) to seek refuge in the United States.

These immigrants brought with them the plant as well. What was different however, is how they used it. They used it as a drug for recreational purposes. The name came by as a negative association of how the Mexicans (who by the way were not liked very much) used the plant.

Later on, when people started associating the name Marijuana with vices like homicides, illicit sex, and theft, through means like films, social stigma towards marijuana became even stronger. This is what even led to the government banning Marijuana.

Even to this day, the name Marijuana hasn't disappeared and many people still associate it with all the negative things.

The Difference

The real difference however between the two plants lies in the amount of a compound contained in both plants called a cannabinoid.

You need to understand that in this regard, there are at least 113 cannabinoids contained in Cannabis. However, the main ones are Tetrahydrocannabinol, otherwise known as THC, and Cannabidiol or CBD.

CBD has very many useful applications, most of which we will look at in the chapters to come. In fact, these useful applications are what have led to the wide acceptance of Cannabis.

THC, on the other hand, is a cannabinoid that is known to have a psychoactive effect on you, once it is in your system. In other words, THC is what causes you to feel "high".

The important thing is to understand that Hemp contains less THC than Marijuana. Hemp is known to contain lesser than 0.3% THC. Marijuana, on the other hand, can contain up to 30% THC. That is where the main difference between the two lies.

It's a little like comparing the characteristics between two oranges. You may find that one orange has more of a sweet taste. However, after tasting another orange, you find that the taste is a little bit sour.

The two oranges both belong to the same family, genus, species and even the physical appearance is the same. They also have the same properties in that they can both be sweet and sour at the same time. However, upon tasting, you find that one orange has more of a sour taste than the other. It is the same thing with hemp and marijuana.

But there is another difference between the two plants...

Cultivation

Given the fact that both plants are grown for different purposes, they do not share similarities in how they are cultivated. Hemp thrives under different conditions than that of Marijuana.

Marijuana is grown in a highly controlled environment. The goal is to produce female plants that have flowers that are budding. In order to ensure a high probability of these characteristics, close measures are taken.

The farmer has to grow the plant under specific conditions such as humidity, temperature and lighting. Also, he or she needs to pay close attention to the plant during its life cycle in order to get things right.

Because of this strictness in the way the plant is handled, you will often find the plant being grown indoors, especially if it is for commercial purposes.

Growing Hemp is a much, much different undertaking. The important thing in growing hemp is to ensure it attains its maximum size as well as yield. Therefore, you will often find the plant being grown outdoors. Also, you do not have to pay as much attention to detail as you would with Marijuana. You can often be sloppy and still get away with it.

Is There A Difference Between CBD Extracted From Both Plants?

Another question that bothers many people is whether there is a difference between CBD extracted from Hemp and that extracted from Marijuana. You may think that given the difference between the two plants, there could be a difference in the CBD as well.

This is a reasonable assumption but unfortunately the answer is, "No. There is no difference."

CBD is CBD regardless of its source. That is what the Chief Scientist at Mary's Nutritionals explains. Both plants can produce high amounts of CBD and there is no difference between the extracts.

The relationship between Marijuana and Hemp is quite complicated and not everyone is sure of the facts. This is probably why Cannabis isn't legalized at a federal level. However, as people become more and more educated, this is going to change.

It is my hope that you now already understand the difference between the two so that you can avoid confusion. Let us now look at the each cannabinoid in turn, including one that is quite unpopular but that is slowly coming to light.

ABOUT CBD AND THC

At this point, you already have an idea of what cannabinoids are. You also know a thing or two about CBD and THC. What you don't know are a few specifics that are vital for understanding everything about Cannabis.

So, let us get down to talking about these specifics.

About Cannabinoids

As I have stated severally, CBD and THC are cannabinoids.

But what are cannabinoids exactly? Good question.

Well, simply put, cannabinoids are nothing but naturally occurring chemicals that are present in plants belonging to the Cannabis genus. They were first discovered in the 1960s by Israeli scientists. It turns out; there are over 113 hundred of them.

However, the ones of the most significance to people like you and me are just a few. CBD and THC top that list. But that isn't all...

The Chemical Composition Of CBD And THC

It may surprise you to realize that CBD and THC – although very different in what they accomplish – are very similar in molecular structure.

Yes, according to CBDorgin.com, they both have 21 atoms made up of carbon, 2 atoms of oxygen and 30 atoms made of hydrogen. In other words, they are nothing short of twins.

So, what accounts for their stark difference?

The difference lies in the arrangement of a single atom. That's all there is – as single atom. If you can't seem to make sense of what I am saying, perhaps the diagram below can make you spot that minute difference.

Cannabidiol   Tetrahydrocannabinol

Now that you have the knowledge of what causes the difference, let me now move on to explain something else.

How it is that THC causes you to become psychoactive while CBD does something else or the complete opposite? The answer lies in how they interact with the endocannabinoid system in your body.

The Endocannabinoid System

Understanding how cannabinoids affect you begins with knowing about the presence of what is known as the endocannabinoid system.

This is a system that consists of a network of receptors that are distributed around the body in every organ. They serve to help your body regulate its health and achieve a stable environment within yourself.

Of these receptors, two are the most important. They are CB1 and CB2 receptors. CB1 receptors are located in regions of the brain. They support functions like memory, cognition and motor coordination. CB2 receptors, on the other hand, are distributed around the nervous and immunity systems.

CBD and THC interact with these receptors differently.

Let's begin by examining how THC interacts with them.

How THC Reacts With The Endocannabinoid System

When you ingest THC, it binds itself directly to CB1 receptors causing them to react. The primary role here is that THC acts as an agonist (or activator). In response, the receptors allow blood flow to an area of the brain, called the prefrontal cortex, to be increased.

This is the area that is responsible for decision making and motor functioning, among others. The effect of this increased blood flow is what makes you feel intoxicated or high.

How CBD Reacts With The Endocannabinoid System

When you ingest CBD, it does something else. Unlike THC, CDB doesn't bind itself directly to the receptors. As a matter of fact, it is an antagonist. What I mean, is that the presence of CBD can counter the effects of THC. This can lower or even eliminate the intoxicating effect caused by THC. The effect of CBD can result in other healthy effects to the body, which we will look at later on.

Next, let us look at another cannabinoid that isn't quite as popular as these two, but one which is slowly gaining attention. That cannabinoid is THCV.

About THCV

There is yet another cannabinoid that is slowly becoming of interest to the Cannabis fraternity.

The question is; **what is it and why should you pay attention to it?**

Let's talk about it.

As you well know, THC and CBD aren't the only cannabinoids in existence. There are many, many others. THCV is one of them.

As the name suggests, you may infer that it is closely related to THC. You would be right to make that assumption.

THCV in full stands for Tetrahydrocannabivarin. It is similar in structure molecularly to THC. It also has mild psychoactive capabilities.

However, the important thing isn't to look at how similar THCV is similar to THC. There are unique capabilities that this cannabinoid has.

Legal Cannabis Will Be Bigger Than Cryptos

One of the most popularized ones is that it can act as an appetite suppressant. There aren't clear explanations of how it accomplishes this but it would be safe to assume that it interacts with the endocannabinoid. This can be a good benefit for people who are looking to lose weight. However, people who have eating disorders like bulimia and anorexia are advised to stay away from it.

One more thing; this cannabinoid is present in very little amounts. Therefore, the only way you can ingest it is together with others like CBD and THC. It's also very difficult to find this cannabinoid in many strains of cannabis. However, it is suggested that you can find higher amounts of it in African strains of Cannabis.

This marks the end of our discussion about cannabinoids. Let us now move past the basics and talk about why your investment in Cannabis is likely to endure for longer. Unlike cryptocurrencies – which people simply bought because prices were going up – Cannabis has some very tangible uses, many of them medical. We will talk about them in a while. But first, let's discuss the various CBD products.

Types Of CBD Products

Previously, we have talked about how the legal cannabis industry is already booming.

The question is; have you stopped to ask yourself; what is at the root of all this? My guess is that this has partly been fueled by the wide range of CBD products that have entered the market today.

You would be surprised to find out just how many products people have managed to come up with that are based on cannabis. You have everything from beauty products to vape pens to edibles. This chapter is aimed at making you well-acquainted with these products so that you can see how wide-spread the influence of legalized cannabis has been.

Let's begin.

1: Beauty Products

The first category of products that are CBD- based are beauty products.

There is no shortage of products that belong to this category.

Some of them include:

- Lip balms
- Soaps
- Serums

- Masks
- Beard oils
- Bath bombs
- Toners
- Cleansers
- Shampoos
- Lotions and moisturizing creams

But have you stopped to ask yourself, as I have; why there would be such increase in the number of products in this area? What makes CBD ideal for such applications?

It turns out; there is a good reason for this. Mostly, it has to do with how CBD interacts with your skin.

Let me explain.

The thing is; your skin is considered to be the biggest organ in your body. It is also the place that is considered to have the highest amount of cannabinoid receptors – you know, the ones we talked about previously while discussing THC.

Those receptors are part of a larger system – the endocannabinoid system – which is responsible for controlling functions in the body such as pains, stress, inflammation, sleep, immunity, and others.

So, when CBD is applied to the skin, it interacts with these receptors and activates them. The result is that pain, inflammation, and lipid production is lowered. The net effect of these changes is that acne is reduced. It also reduces the effect of conditions like dry skin, eczema, aging, and psoriasis. Because of these benefits, CBD has been added to all kinds of beauty and skincare products.

2: Oil-Based Capsules

We also have CBD extracts that are packaged in capsule form. They look like a typical supplement capsule. With regards to this, you have two main types of capsules: those that contain an oil-based extract and those that contain the extract in powder form.

You may be curious to know, "What makes up the contents of these capsules?" If that's the case, let's talk about that briefly.

✓ ***CBD extract or CBD isolate***

You may be interested to know that CBD products are made of either extracts or isolates.

But what are they and how different are they from each other? Good question. Let me elaborate.

For one thing, a CBD extract is better known as "full-spectrum" CBD extract. It is an oily substance that has an oily-like appearance. It contains cannabinoids, fatty acids and terpenoids. An extract, which is of high quality preserves all the components of cannabis. For this reason, extracts provide maximum health benefits to the consumer – a phenomenon called the entourage effect.

On the other hand, there is CBD isolate. As the name suggests, it is CBD that has been isolated in its purest form. Unlike CBD extract, it exists in crystalline form, mainly as a powder. 99% of this powder is pure CBD.

Many people regard CBD isolate as the Cannabis of choice because it contains no THC. And therefore, people realize that when tested for drug use, the results will come out negative. Also, it is cheaper than full-spectrum CBD extract.

The problem is, CBD isolate isn't regarded as effective as CBD extract. The isolate lacks fatty acids and terpenoids and therefore, you cannot experience the **"entourage effect"**.

- ✓ **Oil Carriers**

The capsules also contain what is known as a carrier.

The carrier is meant to allow your body to easily absorb cannabinoids. You already know that CBD is not water soluble. So what the carriers do is break the CBD down and bind it to fats. After it is stored in fat, the CBD easily get absorbed by the body.

- ✓ **"Other" ingredients**

After oil carriers, you also have other ingredients that are not necessarily related to Cannabis. These include things such as supplements or herbs. Their addition is always optional, but the main idea is to provide extra health benefits.

But why use oil-based CBD capsules in the first place. The benefits are plenty. Remember, the CBD interaction with the endocannabinoid system is what makes these health benefits a reality. Some of them are:

- Reducing acne
- Helping with depression
- Helping with appetite suppression
- Reducing anxiety
- Helping cure chronic pain

And much more.

3: CBD Concentrates

Another type of CBD products worth your attention are CBD concentrates.

These are nothing but extracts that contain high amounts of CBD. They are particularly good for you especially if you want to consume a high amount of CBD and are looking to experience the effects quickly.

They come in various forms and they depend on the method used to prepare the concentrate as well as the source. They can all be put into four main categories.

They are:

✓ **CBD distillates**

CBD distillates are termed as "top-of-the range" as far as CBD concentrates go. Therefore, they are highly priced. Some reasons are because the distillates contain a high amount of CBD, are versatile and are neutral in taste.

They are mainly prepared through a process of distillation - which is quite complicated but a highly efficient process nevertheless.

✓ **CBD wax**

This is a form of concentrate that is soft and resembles wax. It is thought to contain around 50% to 70% CBD

It is placed in specialized vape pens. It is then heated at a temperature of around 200º C. This makes the wax to vaporize. This vapor is the inhaled by the consumer.

The wax can even be mixed with a carrier oil and placed under the tongue. It can even be mixed with other creams and applied on the skin.

✓ **CBD crumble**

Crumble is a form of CBD concentrate that can have as much as 99% CBD and 0% THC.

It easily crumbles when touched or placed under heat.

Rumble is mainly used in dap as well as concentrate pens.

✓ **CBD isolate**

Lastly, you have CBD isolate. You already know what it is.

Just like CBD crumble, it can contain as much as 99.9% CBD. It is completely devoid of all other cannabinoids or compounds.

It is mainly used to create vape juice. It can also be used in cosmetics.

Let's move on to yet another interesting CBD product.

4: Drinks

We have just seen that ingesting CBD oil through the mouth is one of the best ways to make the most of it.

There is one downside though – CBD isn't water soluble. Even though CBD oils seem to work just fine for most people, it doesn't seem to be the best solution for people who want more.

But why is this case?

You should understand that your body is made of almost 60% water. And you recall that CBD is hydrophobic in nature – it doesn't dissolve in water. This presents a problem when the body is trying to absorb CBD; very little CBD is absorbed to achieve the desired result. This problem is famously referred to as a **low bioavailability**.

To boost bioavailability, more research has been conducted to solve this matter. Today, there is oil that has been refined so much that it is almost compatible with water. This oil has made it possible to increase the absorption of CBD.

Many people (especially those in marketing) have mistakenly referred to it as water soluble CBD. This is misleading information for people like you who are keen on learning the facts.

The important thing though, is that this innovation has led to a wide range of drinks that contain CBD.

They include:

- CBD water
- Beer
- Energy shots
- Powdered drink mixes, and more

5: CBD Edibles

CBD isn't just associated with everything boring; it has a fun side too, and CBD edibles are proof of that fact.

So what are CBD edibles anyway?

They are simply eatable products that you are familiar with such as chocolates, cakes, gummies, cookies, and the like.

How are they created? Well, they are created through the addition of either CBD isolate or CBD extracts during the creations process.

The main feature that makes these products so unique and so important is that they allow you and everyone else to consume CBD with ease. Think about it. How many people (with the exception of diabetics) will have a problem taking cake? Now compare that number with people who will be willing to ingest CBD oil.

But just how effective are these products?

The short answer is: "Not so much." The first reason is that most of these products are created with CBD isolates, which lack the benefits of CBD extracts. At the same time, most of these products are processed by the liver, which reduces the concentration of CBD.

So overall, edibles aren't as effective as you might expect them to be, but you can argue that they are better than nothing.

6: Pet Products

You might be thinking that CBD products can be used by human beings only. I know I did once; until I realized just how wrong I was.

It turns out; CBD is equally beneficial to animals as well. So, if you have a pet at home (or any other animal) and you would like to provide him or her with the numerous benefits of CBD, you are in great luck.

There are plenty of products designed specifically for that purpose. For instance, you can find treats, tinctures, sprays and many other products that contain CBD being offered for sale.

You may be wondering, "Why on earth would I want to give CBD to an animal?" It's a justified concern. But I promise you there are good reasons for that.

For instance, PetMD did one piece highlighting the health benefits of CBD to dogs. Some of the included treatment of the following:

- Seizures
- Nausea
- Stress
- Anxiety
- Arthritis
- Cancer
- Back pain, and many others

So if you have a pet that you are constantly worried about, you may want to find out what CBD products are out there that could do him or her some good.

Let's move on to yet another product.

7: Suppositories

Suppositories are another line of CBD products that you ought to know about.

To be blunt, these are the weirdest CBD products you will ever know about. This is due to their method of administration. However, you shouldn't despise them for that reason. There is a good reason for that, which I will highlight in a minute.

Let's first talk about what they are.

Suppositories are small bullet-shaped pills that are meant to be inserted in the anus. That's correct; the anus. They are lubricated so that the insertion process is easier. Once in place, the contents start finding their way into your bloodstream.

But why resort to such a strange way of ingesting CBD? The reason is simple – **bioavailability.**

We have just talked about how bioavailability is such a big problem, when it comes to making use of other CBD products. It may come as a shock to you to learn that ingestion of suppositories allows for the highest bioavailability of all products.

The moment you place them in your anus, it takes anywhere from 10 to 15 minutes for the contents to be absorbed into your bloodstream. What's more is that the effects of administering CBD this way lasts for approximately 8 hours.

Ingesting CBD by way of suppositories may not be your cup of tea but, the benefits of doing so have proven that it is worth going through the trouble.

8: Oil-Based CBD Tinctures

CBD oil or tinctures are another popular line of CBD products.

The product is always sold in a small bottle along with a dropper. The dropper is used to help you administer the contents.

But what exactly makes up the contents of the tincture? Let's talk about that.

✓ *CBD extract or CBD isolate*

This one should be obvious to you by now. Every product contains one of these; otherwise, the name CBD would not apply. This is the component that provides the medicinal properties of the product. And of course, CBD extract provides far more value than CBD isolate.

✓ *Carrier oil*

Next in line, you have the carrier oil. The carrier oil mostly includes oils like hemp oil or MCT oil. However, other carriers like alcohol and vegetable glycerin are starting to be included as well.

The first reason why it is included is because it helps balance the potency of CBD. The other reason is that it helps in the delivery of CBD as well as other molecules. The idea is to help with the absorption of CBD into the linings of the stomach and other membranes in the body.

✓ *Other additives*

The third component represents additives that are usually optional and so you may not find them in some products.

They are usually added for any number of reasons. Some of them serve as sweeteners while some are simply flavors. It would be safe to assume that most of them are meant to improve the taste of the oil so that you may favor the product.

However, there are those that are added to provide more nutritious value. For instance, you may find that olive oil has been added to provide some of its numerous health benefits.

So how do you ingest CBD oil?

Using the dropper, you simply place the oil below your tongue. You then allow it to remain there for around 1 to 2 minutes before swallowing. The mucous membranes that are present below your tongue will then allow the CBD molecules to find their way into your bloodstream.

From then on, it takes around 20 minutes before the effects of CBD kick in. Such effects can then last for up to 6 hours.

9: Topicals/ Rubs/ Balms

We also have CBD products specifically designed to be applied on the skin.

Previously, we talked about the skin having more endocannabinoid receptors than any other organ in the body. This has provided a reason for people in the CBD industry to develop products that can be applied to it. Some of those products include rubs, balms, salves, and more.

The fact that the skin has a huge number of receptors means that if you feel some pain or irritation in an area of your body that is close to the skin, you could apply one of these products on the area and this would provide relief. This very aspect has made CBD instrumental in creation of massage oils.

Other problems that can be treated by CBD topicals include muscle soreness and skin conditions.

10: Transdermal Patches

There is yet another class of CBD products that is applied to the skin. That class is a transdermal patch. They are different from topicals or balms in that they form a patch that sticks onto the skin.

But what different features do they offer?

They bring about effects that are more long-lasting than those of rubs or balms. They also tend to offer a slow-release of the underlying problem.

This is made possible by the patch. The patch holds the substance onto the skin for long enough for CBD to enter your bloodstream. This makes transdermal patches better than topicals.

These features make them ideal for you, especially if you have been suffering from chronic pain.

But what is the secret behind the effectiveness of transdermal patches? The answer lies with permeation carriers and enhancers. These are components that are included in the product to help CBD get into your bloodstream.

It is important to note that transdermal patches work better when applied in areas where there are more veins.

11: Vape Products

Inhaling CBD is probably the most widely known method of ingesting CBD, and for good reason. It provides a way of ingesting CBD while ensuring a high bioavailability.

There are a number of products that allow you to ingest vaporized CBD. They include:

- ✓ **_Disposable Vape Pens_**

If you are an inexperienced person in the world of CBD, then this may be the right product for you. It gives you the opportunity to test out and see whether you and CBD can get along.

The pen is bought filled with CBD vape oil. The pen also has a battery that is connected to an atomizer. You simply turn it on to inhale the vapor.

If you find that vape CBD isn't the right product for you, then you can simply get rid of the pen.

- ✓ **_Vape Cartridges_**

You can find CBD vape cartridges that are refillable as well as well as those that are disposable. They have batteries that are almost similar to those of vape pens.

Making use of them is quite simple. You simply turn the cartridge towards the end that has the battery. Then you start inhaling the vapor.

- ✓ **_E-liquid_**

Lastly, you have e-liquid, otherwise known as vape juice.

This is simply CBD that has been turned into vapor and then sold off as a product by itself. It is normally packaged in a small bottle that is squeezable or a dropper. If you exhaust the contents, you always have the option of refilling the bottle.

12: Water-Soluble CBD Powder

Lastly, but not the least, there is water-soluble powder.

This is powder that has been designed to dissolve into water as well as anything else such as food, beverages, and more. This provides you as the potential user with a lot of freedom with this type of product.

Now that we have looked at quite a number of CBD products, let us now move on to the main section of this book, where we talk about how you can actually put your money to work for you in this new industry. See you on the other side.

HOW YOU CAN INVEST IN CANNABIS

This book would be useless if I went on and on covering background material on Cannabis without actually focusing on what the book promises in its title. So, in this chapter, I will go into what you have probably been waiting for all along – how you can invest and make money in the Cannabis industry.

Get ready; this is the part where the rubber hits the road.

Are you ready? Good. Let's start by discussing the various reasons why the legal Cannabis industry is a good place to put your money. After all, you wouldn't want to invest in anything without having solid reasons, would you?

Why Invest In Legal Cannabis?

Will investing in legal Cannabis make you rich? Chances are good that it will.

Here's why:

1. *The size of the market*

The first thing that should boost your confidence about Cannabis is the significant size of the market itself. Many investors shy away from new markets terming them as "not big enough to capture my interest." That is not the case with Cannabis.

Although research from various firms depicts different results, one thing is clear, the legal Cannabis industry is valued at tens of billions of dollars.

Legal Cannabis Will Be Bigger Than Cryptos

Take for instance the research conducted by giant Grand View research. According to the firm, the legal Cannabis industry was valued at $13.8 billion by the end of 2018. Further, it is reported that the industry is expected to grow annually at a compound annual growth rate (CAGR) of 23.9% to reach approximately 66.3 billion by 2025.

In addition to that, data from the company shows that the industry has always grown steadily ever since 2014, as shown in the chart below:

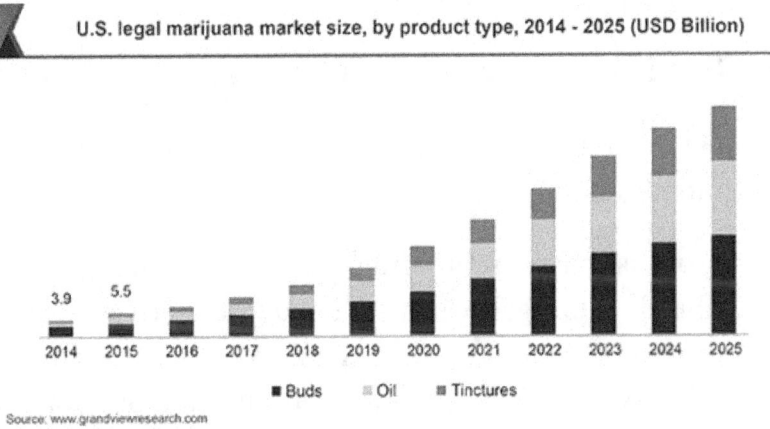

Looking at the data representation above, anyone with experience in forecasting with data analytics would concur that the Cannabis industry isn't likely to slow down any time soon.

And remember, this data belongs to the legal segment of the Cannabis industry alone. If you add up proceeds from both the legal market and the black market, the numbers could easily reach hundreds of billions of dollars.

That is exactly what data from the United Nations Office of Drugs and Crime (UNODC) depicts. They estimate that the Cannabis industry in its entirety could easily be worth $150 billion today.

This number almost rivals that of other popular industries like the carbonated drinks industry, which is expected to grow to $412.5 billion by 2023, at a CAGR of 2.3%. Looking at the CAGR alone, you would be right to agree that it is much better to put your money in Cannabis, than to have it in say, "Coca Cola" or "Pepsi".

2. Decriminalization of Cannabis

Another compelling reason for investing in Cannabis is decriminalization.

Many of us have been afraid of even thinking about Cannabis due its legality state. Nobody wants to get caught on the wrong side of the law. However, this is changing gradually. We have seen a wave of legalization of Cannabis sweep through the United States. It has also touched on other parts of the world.

And as governments become more and more educated on the safety of Cannabis as well as the benefits it can have on humans, you can expect that wave to sweep across the rest of the world in the nearby future.

It would be safe to say that, as of the moment, governments hold the key to the rapid expansion of this industry. They are the ones who wield the power to give the "green light" on commercial activities in this sector. In recent times, governments have indicated that they are willing to do so.

But that's not what's exciting. The exciting thing is the fact that every time the government issues a "go ahead", the industry has shown remarkable improvement in terms of performance. You can think of government approvals as the catalyst of industry growth.

As an investor, you can capitalize on these improvements and reap some huge returns on investment. As an example, when Donald Trump passed the 2018 farm bill that legalized industrial hemp growth, Charlotte's Web Holdings, a major participant in the Cannabis industry, saw the price of its stock go up by 9.17%. You can imagine that was a big day for the investors of the company.

3. *Hemp oil is legal in all 50 states*

We know that marijuana isn't legal nationwide. However, the same can't be said for hemp.

According to the Agricultural Act of 2018, otherwise known as the Far Bill, hemp is legal across the country. This is good news for people in the Cannabis industry since Hemp is the best source of CBD. It is also the source that contains the lowest amount of THC, making it preferable for most people who do not want to get high.

This also means that you can manufacture CBD oil and market it all over the country. You are not limited in terms of your market, as is the case with marijuana. And since there is a high demand of CBD oil, you can expect to get a good return on your investment if you decide to go into the business.

4. Changing public sentiment

Public opinion about Cannabis is just as important. It won't matter if the government legalized Cannabis, while a huge part of the public despise it.

Remember, the public forms the market. All production in the world is done because there is a demand for the product being developed. If the public didn't demand the product or felt that the product wasn't safe, then everything else would need to be stopped.

In the same way, the public holds much sway in the feasibility of the Cannabis industry.

The good news is, the public actually favors the adoption of legalized Cannabis. Earlier, we looked the numbers and determined that a majority of the public support its legalization. This is especially true for people under age 35, who now form a staggering 85%.

If you consider the fact that most millennials form the largest number of buyers of CBD products, this is nothing short of astounding. In fact, one report showed that 50% of millennials would actually prefer CBD oil over mental health prescription drugs.

In short, there is enough backing by the potential buyers of legal Cannabis, to make you consider it safe investment idea.

5. Cannabis stocks are becoming mainstream

We all tend to favor things that are in the mainstream. They tend to provide us with a sense of safety that we usually can't get from things that are hidden in the limelight. For some reasons, we find it hard to trust the newest kids on the block. We aren't sure they will be around for long enough.

The same thing happens in the investment world.

Let me ask you this; would you rather invest in Apple stock or some bizarre company that recently went public? Your answer is obviously as good as mine; Apple seems like the right way to go. As a matter of fact, they are already looking forward to huge sales of their newest line of products – iPhone 11.

In the same way, you (and many others) may mistrust Cannabis stocks because they aren't sure what the future holds for them. They are still lurking in the shadows and without enough traction may stay there and disappear into the abyss.

But that is changing

It was only recently that Cannabis stocks were dealt in the over-the-counter (OTC) market. However, after legalization in the U.S, such stocks are now listing in the New York Stock Exchange; Cronos and Tilray are good examples of such stock. As of this writing, there are more than a dozen companies belonging to the Cannabis industry that are listed in various exchanges in the U.S.

With this kind of exposure, it won't be long before these companies get the attention they deserve – something that you can take advantage of.

6. Mergers and acquisitions are taking place

Mergers and acquisitions are some of the key drivers of company growth in the corporate world. And this can mean a lot for you who is considering investing in the Cannabis industry.

The Cannabis industry has seen at least two major acquisitions, not mentioning huge support and partnerships from other companies with unlimited funds. For instance in 2018, Atlanta Group, a major player in Tobacco bought a 45% stake in Cronos, which is valued at around $ 1.8 billion.

Also, Constellation Brands (an alcohol producer) bought a 37% stake in Canopy Growth. The deal was valued at $4 billion.

Deals like these are what fuel growth in an industry. Think about it, would these companies spend such vast sums to buy large stakes in Cannabis if they didn't have to? You are right, they wouldn't. This should be a sign that you can forge ahead with confidence.

In addition, events like these are big news for the companies involved (especially the target company).

According to Investopedia, in the period before and after a merger or acquisition, the value of stock of the target company usually goes up, sometimes significantly.

You can stand to reap huge returns if this happens to a company that you have bought stakes in. There has never been a better time to buy shares in Cannabis stocks than now since there are only a handful of them in the market right now. You can analyze some good companies with great potential and invest in them.

Chances are, somewhere down the road, a major Alcohol, Cigarette, Pharmaceutical or Food Company may step in and offer a deal that can't be refused and this could work out in your favor.

7. Wall Street analysts are paying more attention

It is no secret that financial analysts – especially those who appear on TV – hold a lot of influence on the marketplace. Many people pay attention to them and take their opinions very seriously. If they vouch for a company, or an industry, you can bet that investors will start flocking that place.

However, these "fairy godmothers" have paid little attention to the Cannabis industry in the past, if at all. Perhaps they deemed the industry unimportant back then.

Not anymore.

More and more attention is being paid to this industry now than ever before. As we speak, crème de la crème firms like Jefferies, Cowen & Co., Piper Jaffray and others are now doing their homework on Cannabis stocks. CNN even once reported that 13 analysts were covering Canopy Growth alone.

Evidence of the power of analysts came to light once when, the share price of Canopy Growth went up by 13% after Piper Jaffray decided to start looking into the cannabis industry. They joined a list of other brokers who were already doing the same.

As this list of analysts looking into this industry keeps growing, big money will make its way into Cannabis fueling growth even further - another good sign.

8. Newer health discoveries

Speculation alone can drive prices to significant levels. We saw that with cryptocurrencies and the legendary Dutch Tulip mania. But speculation alone isn't the key driving factor.

The real value of the underlying financial instrument determines price movement as well. That is why companies' share prices go up when earnings reports show up better than the previous quarter when a company takes credit of developing a new form of technology.

In each of these cases, the price went up because, in the eyes of investors, the company's stock had become more valuable.

The same thing happens with Cannabis. New discoveries are made every now and then about the medical benefits of CBD. These CBD benefits are announced to the public every now and then. They are like financial reports from companies and so you can expect investors to push prices further.

Take for instance, the drug Epidiolex, which was approved by the FDA in 2018, which was meant to treat patients with seizures and epilepsy. The drug contains CBD and costs around $32,500 per patient every year. There a good chance that the pharmaceutical company that developed this drug will rake in huge bucks as a result of this new drug going public.

News like these tend to excite investors and improve their confidence in their investment.

9. *There are many ways to participate in this market*

Lastly, but not the least, the Cannabis industry is attractive because it offers many different ways to participate in it.

Yes, and we will look into some of those ways in this chapter. You may be thinking that entering this market will be difficult but I assure you it isn't. Buying stocks and growing Cannabis may be some of the best ways to make money in this industry, but they are not your only options.

There are several easier and far-cheaper ways of operating in the Cannabis industry that could turn a handsome profit for you (and even a nice living) if you give them a chance.

This isn't always a benefit that comes easy and in any industry. I know of countless industries that ordinary people like you and I will never afford to participate, and which - despite the financial barrier - are still loaded with risk. But with Cannabis, at least you stand a chance.

Now that we are done looking at the various economic reasons why you should consider investing in this wonderful market, let us now get to the meat of this chapter and talk about how you can start making money.

How To Ride The Cannabis Wave: To Make Money In The Cannabis Industry

Some of these ideas may not resonate with you. If that's the case, you can simply disregard them and look into the next one. My hope is to provide you with enough choices so that you can explore the options that suit you best.

Now, without further ado, let's dig in.

#1. Starting a Cannabis blog

One of the easiest ways to break into the Cannabis market is to start a blog. It is cheap to start and probably won't cost you a lot of money to run if you perform your due diligence. Plus, there is a lot of information to help you whenever you get stuck.

But why try it in the first place?

Let me explain a few good reasons...

Hot topic

Anybody who has operated a successful business on the web will tell you how important hot topics are.

Hot topics represent what the public is currently interested in. They show what people are actively searching about. And that has a lot of business value. It wouldn't do you any good to set up a business on something that no one is interested in.

Hot topics are so valuable, they are one of the most accurate ways of determining supply and demand on the web. In fact, an entire industry has thrived for long for this reason – keyword research.

The important thing for you to realize right now is that Cannabis and its related terms like marijuana are classified as some of the most frequently searched terms at the moment. Mondovo, a digital marketing giant, lists "marijuana" in its list of the most frequently searched terms of 2019. This alone should make you consider venturing into blogging about Cannabis.

Insufficient information

Also, there isn't enough information on the subject. In fact, I can guarantee you that this book is one of the few reliable sources you will find right now on Cannabis.

At the time of this writing, there are a few blogs that have information about marijuana that is correct, useful and comprehensive. Many of them have a few pieces, but not the whole thing. Today, if you started on a mission to gather as much information on Cannabis as possible, you would run into many closed avenues and would have to break quite a sweat.

This is a huge gap for an area that has gained so much public interest. This is in stark contrast to other areas like "digital marketing" and "online business". There are many well-established brands that have already cornered those markets. You wouldn't make it in those areas as a newcomer with limited resources.

Nonetheless, there is tremendous opportunity for you to set up shop in Cannabis. Apparently, not many people have turned their attention toward it. But given enough time, I can guarantee you they will.

And as an entrepreneur, it is up to you to exploit gaps like these before more people do. By going through the trouble of providing as much accurate information on marijuana as possible, you increase the likelihood of establishing yourself as an authority in this new and exciting industry – the go to guy of information on Cannabis.

Think about it. How exciting would it be for you to claim such a rare spot? Are you happy now that you even chose to read this book?

So how exactly do you take advantage of this option? We are going to talk about that from start to finish. By the time you are done reading this, you will be ready to get started right away with no qualms.

Successfully starting a blog and making money from it requires that you go through a set of steps. Those steps are:

Step 1: Choosing a name for your blog

This is a crucial first step that you would need to go through. You may think that this is a no-brainer but I assure you it isn't.

Success in blogging depends on many things and picking the right name for your blog is an important one. If you choose the wrong name for your blog (and business for that matter), you will be stuck with it forever and will struggle to get the attention and status that you deserve.

Take a look at the following blog names from different industries:

- Copyblogger   -   Blogging and copywriting
- Problogger   -   Blogging
- Content Marketing Institute - Content marketing
- Search Engine Land   -   Search Engine Optimization
- Cryptocurrencyfacts   -   Cryptocurrencies

The first thing that you realize is that the names speak for themselves even before anything. A first glance at the name and you immediately know what these blogs are all about. And keep in mind; these blogs are all authorities (industry leaders) in their own right.

What does this tell you? It's simple, if you ever hope to model these blogs in the Cannabis industry, you would need to come up with a name that is relevant and descriptive, as these are. I will leave the rest up to you. Let's move on.

Step 2: Registering and getting hosting

After coming up with a name for your blog that you are satisfied, you will need to register for a domain name and get hosting for your website.

Legal Cannabis Will Be Bigger Than Cryptos

In case you have never heard of it before, a domain name is nothing but the name that your website visitors will need to type into their browsers to find you. You know like **"Facebook.com"** or **"Google.com"**? You get the point.

The thing is, your domain name cannot be the same as that of someone else. That is where it gets tricky. You may have come up with a cute name like **"thecannabisblog.com"**, but unless you were the first one to come up with that name and secured it, you will not own it.

For this reason, there are places where you can search whatever domain name you come up with to make sure that it is available. Once you find one that is, you will be presented with an option to purchase it (you can easily spend a lot of time on this step). One such place that is my favorite is at the website of hosting giant GoDaddy.

Once you purchase your domain name, you will need to purchase hosting. Hosting ties your domain name to a server where your website files will reside. The good thing is that most areas you purchase your domain name also provide hosting as a service, so you can place your order for both and get over it with.

Don't worry; your hosting company will actually go through the trouble of configuring the technical details about your website. They will contact you with the necessary details about logging in and accessing your website's control panel. They can even install blogging software at your request. There are several blogging software out there but WordPress maintains its reputation as the best. It is also free.

Step 3: Choosing a design for your blog

After registering your domain name and getting hosting, you should be ready for the next step – choosing a design.

A design is simply the layout of your blog. You can hire a professional designer to develop a custom design for you but I assure you that won't be necessary.

Assuming you installed WordPress as your software of choice, you will be happy to find out that WordPress repository has an endless catalogue of both free as well as premium design templates or themes (as they like to call them). You can check some of the free ones here. Premium themes are found in other third party marketplaces like Themeforest and Envato Market. You will have to pay for the premium ones but I assure you they aren't expensive.

Many of them are built for blogging but there are other special themes for special types of businesses. Your interest is in blogging so you should only stick to those.

The process of installing a theme on WordPress should be as easy as clicking install from the catalog or repository if you are browsing for free themes. But, installation of premium themes is a bit more complicated and you might have to call in a professional in case you find it difficult to understand the technicalities.

Nevertheless, they come with plenty of documentation that should be able to walk you through literally every step of the way.

Step 4: Creating content

Once you have your design in place, your next step is creating content.

This is the most important step in this venture and one that you will have to go on with for as long as you are willing to stay in this business.

So how do you craft content that is crisp, of high quality and engaging at the same time? What style is the best? How do you decide what to write and what not to write? Which topics are worth exploring?

Well, it's a tough science and there are no clear rules. It is also an endless maze and many times, the rules do change as time goes by. Most of the time, whatever you decide will depend on how well you know your audience (or blog readers), among other factors. But covering the ins and outs of content creation is beyond the scope of this book.

The good thing is, there are many resources created to help you with that. One good resource I know is Epic Content Marketing. It is written by Joe Pulizzi who is also the CEO of Content Marketing Institute. There is plenty of solid expert advice in there that can help you.

Step 5: Promoting your blog

Creating great content is good, but by itself, isn't very effective. Like any other business, you will also need to promote the content you develop as well as your blog. After all, without traffic, you wouldn't have readers, and without readers, you wouldn't create an audience, and without and audience, you wouldn't have customers.

Promotion is a must in blogging but there are no hard and fast rules. Some things you could try include:

- Guest blogging on other popular Cannabis blogs
- Commenting on social media pages and groups related to Cannabis and linking back to your blog
- Publishing content on Medium.com and linking back to your blog
- Answering questions about Cannabis on Quora.com and linking back to your site
- Using lead magnets like eBooks on Cannabis to capture emails subscribers
- Partnering with other Cannabis websites to create powerful content
- Sharing content on Twitter
- Paid advertising on social media
- Search marketing, and others

But, keep in mind that there is no single formula for success. There are timeless tactics that have continued to perform well for those that have tried, but there are also others that simply no longer work.

Also, whatever works for one niche or industry may not work for another. For instance, I know of high-traffic blogs that rely primarily on social media for traffic but haven't invested seriously in Search Engine Optimization.

Again, like I said; sometimes figuring out the details of what truly works can at times feel like rocket science. The important thing is to keep going on and testing whatever you think might work and letting go of what doesn't. In the world of content marketing, there is no single formula that works for everybody.

Nonetheless, you can get pretty far if you diligently do the work and take your time. At the very least, it may take you a couple of years before you grow to become a major player. But once you get there, the results are worth the effort.

I am saying that because content marketing is slowly becoming the most powerful method of marketing; even more powerful than advertising. In fact, it is so powerful that some of the biggest companies in the world are restructuring their marketing efforts to comply with it.

Step 6: Monetizing your blog

After working so hard to create great content about Cannabis on your blog that educates and resonates with your readers and ensuring that you have a large enough audience that is loyal to you, you will need to monetize your blog so that you can create a business.

Remember your goal is to run a profitable business, not to perform charity work - which is what you will be doing if you fail to monetize your blog.

So how do you turn your audience into buying customers?

Joe Pulizzi says that this is always the easiest part. "*Once you have grown a large enough audience, you can then sell whatever you want to that audience.*"

There are many monetizing strategies out there that you could try.

Some of the best ones include:

- Providing links to Cannabis products on an affiliate basis
- Selling books of your own about cannabis
- Selling courses of your own on Cannabis
- Advertising Cannabis products on your blog
- Selling your blog for profit

This is the end game in blogging. However, you can never get here without going through the initial steps first. In blogging, there are no shortcuts. It's good, old fashioned, "hard-earned money". You only truly reap what you sow, and you must have patience

Let's look at other methods of making money in the Cannabis industry.

#2. Open A Cannabis Dispensary

Another lucrative option you can explore is that of opening a Cannabis dispensary.

But what is a Cannabis dispensary by definition?

A Cannabis dispensary is a place – typically a storefront – which operates legally, the business of selling both medical as well as recreational Cannabis products.

In other words, a Cannabis dispensary is the place where you visit, when you want purchase a Cannabis vape pen, Cannabis edible, CBD oil or any one of those products we discussed in a previous chapter of this book. Another word for a Cannabis dispensary would be a Cannabis shop or Cannabis Cooperative.

Opening one of them is a great way of investing in the Cannabis industry and can be very profitable indeed, if you are willing to put in the time and the effort. That's right; this is what Marijuana Business Daily tells us. According to a report they did, sales from marijuana dispensaries are expected to exceed $6.5 billion in 2019.

Think for a minute. Wouldn't you want a piece of that pie? I know I do. But wait, not so fast. There is plenty of work to do upfront, and plenty still to be done afterwards. Hopefully, with a little guidance from this book, you will lay the proper groundwork so that you can get started. Just like with blogging, we will go over a series of steps that you can cover to get much of the initial work done.

Step 1: Take a hard look at your eligibility as well as your commitment

You start by performing a self-assessment. Are you committed to push past the hurdles in this business so that you can make it?

Are you eligible under the law to go into this business?

Those are the questions you need to begin with.

There is this misguided notion out there that you can get into the Cannabis industry to make a quick buck. If you have been operating under that false assumption, you need to snap out of it as first as you can.

If you go into ahead and open a Cannabis dispensary with this mindset, you will surely be setting yourself for a lot of disappointment down the road. As you will see, in the steps below, there is no "easy money" in Cannabis. If you are the type to disappear at the first sign of trouble, then you had better toughen up or get rid of the idea from your mind.

That is what Mitch Woolhiser, who has operated successfully in this business since 2010, advises as well. This is what he says, *"If the only reason why you are getting into this is money, then you are not going to have a good time. It is not a get rich quick scheme. It's a long game. You have to have to have something that motivates you."* You would be wise to take his words to heart.

Take some time and ask yourself, "What is my true intention of going into this business?" "Am I going in just to make a quick buck or am I willing to take all the responsibility and run it professionally?" "Will I be here 10,

20, 30, perhaps 50 years from now?" "Am I genuinely interested in this idea? Do I have the drive, the passion?"

Questions like these will force you to clarify your thinking and get your facts right.

What follows after this is a question of eligibility. Not everyone is qualified to start a Cannabis dispensary. For one thing, if you have a past criminal record, you cannot lay your hands on this idea. Background checks are a requirement by the organizations that are tasked with licensing you.

I addition to that, your investors as well as employees will also need to be vetted before they can be involved in your business. If you have a clean slate, then you have nothing to worry about and should probably move on to the next step.

Step 2: Conduct research and consult on legal matters

The cannabis industry is very shaky ground, legally speaking, and there is need for you to tread carefully. Failing to get a few legal facts right could put you in a lot of trouble with the authorities. For this reason, it is vital that your research in this area is thorough.

For one thing, if you are serious about going into this business, you will need to be well acquainted with the laws concerning Cannabis, both locally and at a federal level. Getting your hands on the Cole memorandum would be a great way to get started. This is the document, which attorneys consult whenever they want to enforce laws on Cannabis. It's indispensable.

However, by itself, this document isn't enough; you will need to visit the legal department in your state and request for legal documentation on Cannabis. The National Organization for the Reform of Marijuana laws (NORM) owns a database that lists side by side the laws regarding marijuana for every state as well as the penalties. This can also come in handy.

Despite all this work, it would be better if you brought in a professional. Having a lawyer go over all the legal matters concerning your decision to open a Cannabis dispensary can be the easiest and safest thing you might do in this situation. There are things that you and I may overlook that an experienced lawyer may not.

Furthermore, you may be too busy handling other matters to even bother going over mountains of legal paperwork. It would be better to get an opinion from someone who practices law for a living while seeking to only getting a basic understanding of the laws yourself.

Fortunately for you, the NORML database lists lawyers who have specialized in the Marijuana industry. Contacting lawyers on this list can save you a lot of headache regarding this matter.

Let's move on.

Step 3: Rent a base of operation

Unless you plan on selling your products online (which we will look into in a bit), you will need to get a physical location to operate your business. This is the step that can prove to be a little tough for you.

To begin, you will need to open up your shop in an area that receives the most traffic; otherwise, your venture may not succeed. On the other hand, there are distinct rules on areas where you are allowed to set up shop.

For instance, in the state of California, some of the laws governing the opening of a Cannabis dispensary include the following:

- Your shop should not be located within 1000 feet of a child care center, or pre-school for that matter.
- It should also not be located within 500 feet of a residential area.
- It should not be within 1000 feet of a library or library
- It should not be within 250 feet of an adult business selling drug paraphernalia e.g. bongs and pipes.

Locating vacant commercial rental buildings that meet these requirements can be tough at best. And if you do find a few that are available, chances are, their rent prices will be sky-high. You will then have to weigh in your options and determine whether it will be worth the risk.

As if that isn't enough, you will also have to deal with landlords who do not share your opinions about Cannabis.

Some of them may turn down your offer once they realize that you intend to operate a Cannabis dispensary.

Mitch Woolsier remembers going through this tough ordeal, "Some landlords just didn't want to deal with it and still won't." "Some of that is because of the federal illegality of marijuana and the liability that they might have."

You may even find that the landlords are under pressure from law enforcement agencies. Lincoln Fish, who has also been in this business for years, is quoted as saying:

> "The DEA sent out letters to landlords all over the country and s we decide to come down on these guys, you can be liable if you are them.'"

After that, one landlord that hosted him kicked him out.

So, it is understandable that if your landlords get threats like these, you can expect that many of them won't put themselves on the line for you.

These are some of the challenges that you may run into while seeking a place to operate your business. You may need to search for property in the company of a lawyer who may explain the legality of what you plan to do to skeptical landlords. It could make your life easier.

Step 4: Create a business plan

Running a Cannabis dispensary is serious business. At the very least, you will have to create a business plan before you get started on crucial matters.

If you have never created a business plan before, you can consult the services of professionals who specialize in that kind of thing. Bplans.com is one place you can depend on for such a kind of service.

Mitch Woolsier relied on them to create a business plan for himself way back in 2010. Considering that he has been in the business for that long, you can expect that their services are worth it.

However, if you decide to consult with another company on this matter, at least make sure your business plan covers the following:

i) *Source of capital*

To be blunt, the Cannabis dispensary business is capital-intensive. This isn't the type of business to go into if you are low on cash and are looking to scrimp and save a few dollars here and there.

For instance, getting a license may cost you as much as $15,000. Remember this is without accompanying legal documents. If you consider other upfront costs, you could be looking at some serious money. Mitch remembers putting up $50,000 and it wasn't enough. He had to borrow some more money from his credit cards and from his family.

He explains that today, you may need as much as $500,000 just to get started, if you adjust for inflation and take into account the fact that there is more competition now.

Even worse, banks cannot advance credit facilities to you because marijuana is illegal federally. Your best hope is to depend on angel investors, family, relatives, close friends, and contacts to raise the needed funds.

ii) Budget

Your plan will also need to include a rough estimate of the money you will need upfront as well as the running costs. You will need to be as clear as possible when it comes to this. Check with wholesalers in your area so that you can determine the prices.

In addition to the cost of buying goods from suppliers, you will also need to account for:

- Rent
- Cost of license
- Cost of license application
- Salaries to employees
- Transportation and storage costs
- Security, and the like

If you work with a professional, you will be able to get most of these things covered.

iii) Know your competition

In business, you will always have competition. The least you can do is know a thing or two about them so that you can develop appropriate strategies.

The saddest part is that most of your competition may come from unlicensed criminal operators. These people pay no tax, social security for employees or even licensing fees to the local, or even the federal government. As such, many of them have an advantage over you. Also, many of them operate round the clock, for 24 hours.

Knowing about them, who they are and what you can do about them, is critical to your survival in this business, according to Mitch.

In reality, competition depends on how you look at it. If you look at it from a negative perspective, it will do you no good. One business course I attended taught me that competition is good because it shows you that whatever you are selling is in demand. Take a look at the most lucrative industries; competition is fierce, always. In fact, a lack of competition is often a sign that there isn't enough demand for your product.

iv) Market research

At the end of the day, you will need to sell products if you run a business. As such, you will need to know your market.

Who will be your customers? What is their demographic? What is their psychographic? How will you reach them? Is your product in high demand?

Information like this is invaluable to a business person. It helps you determine strategy as well as pricing.

BPlans actually offers a free template for a Cannabis dispensary business plan. You can download it here so that you go over the things needed to come up with your own.

Step 5: Acquire your license

Your next step is to make sure you acquire the necessary license.

We have already looked at some details about this step. A quick look at the documentation of the State of Colorado can provide you with an idea of what needs to be done. The important thing is to understand that you may have to involve a legal professional in this process. As such, you must be prepare to cough up some hefty fees.

You will also need to have a lawyer on stand-by as you run your business, so that they can keep you up to date on legal matters as well as defend you should the need arise.

Step 6: Source great product

You wouldn't want to go through the above steps and then mess things up in the sourcing of product. You will have to check out sources that provide products of high quality and diversity.

Some dispensaries even take things a notch higher by cultivating their own marijuana. As a beginner, this may not be necessary but as time goes, you may find out the importance of doing so. Keep in keep in mind that in some states, operating your own marijuana farm is mandatory.

However, Mitch confirms that there are plenty of suppliers in this industry so much of the legwork has been done for you. You just have to establish contact.

Step 7: Conduct marketing

So you have done your homework, secured a place, even procured some high quality product and stocked your shelves.

What next?

You will need marketing. Every business does, especially in the early stages.

The truth is; marketing is a deep subject and you may have to read some books and maybe enroll in some business classes, or recruit professionals to help you with it.

This book unfortunately doesn't go into the specifics of doing that. But there are plenty of resources out there to help you out.

Step 8: Invest in security

Also, you will need to invest in security. Operating a Cannabis dispensary can be profitable and as with any profitable business, security is a must.

Also, remember you will be operating a cash business since banks are reluctant to take money from marijuana operators, as it is illegal federally. Therefore, most of the time, you will have cold hard cash in the premises. This makes you a juicy target for criminals.

You must protect yourself, your employees as well as your investment. You cannot afford to tolerate any laxity in security matters.

Step 9: Stay informed

Lastly, the legal environment surrounding the marijuana industry is always changing. There's no telling what tomorrow holds.

As a business person, you will need to keep your ear on current developments. You do not want to get caught off-guard. Do your best to follow the news and have your lawyer on speed dial.

Moving on, let us look at another option – becoming an edibles chef.

#3. Become And Edibles Chef

Investing in a career in becoming an edibles chef can also be a lucrative option in the long run. You see, everybody has to eat at the end of the day. So chefs have always been always in demand. And that isn't likely to change any time soon.

The culinary arts have always been an ever-expanding industry and with the introduction of Cannabis edibles, you can curve out a niche for yourself.

Let us look at a few aspects of becoming a cannabis edibles chef so that you are better informed on this opportunity.

Who is a Cannabis Chef?

Let's start by talking about who a Cannabis Chef is and what he or she does.

In simple terms, a Cannabis Chef is person who prepares food and drinks that are infused with either THC or CBD.

In a previous chapter, we talked about edibles being part of a line of Cannabis products that you ought to know of. For instance, there are sweets, cakes, cookies, chocolates and the like. A Cannabis Chef prepares those products.

A Cannabis Chef typically works in commercial kitchens. It is the job of a Cannabis chef to ensure that the consumables are well prepared, packaged and labeled with accurate potency information.

Now that you understand who a Cannabis chef is and what he or she does at work, let us move on and talk about the education behind such a wonderful career.

Getting the education you need

Since the Cannabis Chef is a relatively new field, there isn't a well laid out educational path in this career. In order to understand how you can actually become a Cannabis chef, you have to start by looking at the typical educational background of a traditional chef.

To start, chefs usually pursue a postsecondary training program in the culinary arts. This program may involve a Certificate, Associate's degree or a Bachelor's degree from an institution offering it.

Some of the things covered include sanitation, safety, nutrition, menu planning as well as meal preparation skills. After attending in-class programs, the student must also complete an internship program that puts their skills to the test.

If after completing a traditional training as a Chef, you want to specialize in the Cannabis industry, you may attend Cannabis cooking classes. Programs like these are available in various cities in States where Marijuana is legal.

You may even want to attend a training program in cannabis science. These programs cover many things, among them: cultivation of cannabis, extraction of isolates and extracts, the effects of Cannabis, infusion and other things.

As you can see, it's a matter of taking a traditional Chef training program, and then later on backing it with specialized training in Cannabis. There is no training in existence that is dedicated to producing Cannabis Chefs specifically.

But is everyone cut out for these programs? Let us take a brief look at the legal requirements.

The legal requirements

Thankfully, there are few barriers to entry in this profession, if at all.

For starters, you must be 20 years of age if you expect to receive Cannabis training. Also, you can only work in areas where marijuana has been legalized for recreational purposes or medical purposes, or both. You will need to obtain legal paperwork such as a food handler's card.

Besides these, there isn't much to go on in this regard. But, be sure to check with a legal professional just to be sure.

Skills you must have

When considering job positions as a Cannabis Chef, if you have been well trained, there are certain skills that you are expected to possess.

They include:

- Outstanding culinary skills
- Ability to work with various kitchen equipment e.g. processors, mixers, ovens, range tops and more.
- Creativity to come up with unique products
- Creative ways to infuse marijuana in beverages and foods
- Ability to carry out complex extraction procedures like CO_2.

Career prospects and potential pay

So, what will you be expecting as you consider this career path?

Well, there's plenty to look forward to. For instance, it is estimated that Chefs and Head cooks look to make anywhere between $50,000 to $100,000 a year, depending on their skill level as well as experience. This number also depends on who your employer is.

Also, the industry is rife with opportunities. For instance, New Frontier Data has estimated that the industry is likely to employ over 200,000 people by the year 2020. Forbes reports that this number is higher than what is expected of the manufacturing industry (which is expecting a nosedive by the way).

In other words, you are better of choosing to go into the Marijuana industry as compared to going into manufacturing.

What holds for the future?

The worst mistake you can make is look to facts that only point to the here and now and neglect what the future holds.

The good news is, becoming a Cannabis Chef holds much promise. A key indicator to look for is the number of states, and countries that are likely to legalize Cannabis in the future.

Once legalization takes place, you can expect that the demand for Cannabis Chefs will go up and so will the potential pay. You can even become a Cannabis Chef instructor and earn even earn more when that happens.

If you consider possibilities like these, you may find that there has never been a better time to become a Cannabis chef.

That's it for becoming a Cannabis edibles chef; let's move on to something else.

#4. Run A Cannabis Lab

Another potentially lucrative investment opportunity in the Cannabis industry is to open a testing lab.

But why start one? Good question.

First of all, understand that the government legalizing Cannabis alone isn't enough for business. The law also requires that products be tested and certified before they can be sold to the public.

They will need testing to make sure that they are of the right quality and safe for consumers as well. For this reason, testing labs are a very important participant and a lucrative opportunity for entrepreneurs.

However, if this option feels like a long shot, it's because it is. This is an option that requires careful evaluation and assessment before you jump into it. Also, you may need to have deeper pockets to pull it off as well.

We are going to go over some things you may need to consider if you intend to take on the challenge of setting up a Cannabis Lab.

Let's begin.

Step 1: Understand the legality

You will have to start at the beginning, and that beginning is understanding just how legal is it for you to set up a Cannabis lab?

Marijuana is illegal federally but hemp is. What is your intention? Do you plan on focusing on Cannabis entirely, hemp or just marijuana? The laws do not apply in the same way, so you need to get clear on that.

Things may not be as black and white as you mistakenly assume, so it is better to check and double-check legal facts. Some states may present different legal requirements as compared to others. Do our best to keep that in mind. Otherwise, your new exciting venture can easily turn into a nightmare.

Also, be sure to ask for the services of a lawyer. I can't imagine anyone navigating the Cannabis industry without one.

As for local regulations within your state, there some things that you may have to meet.

Some of them include the following:

i) ISO/IEC accreditation

This accreditation is meant to prove that you are competent to carry out Cannabis testing activities. It also serves to dictate the standard procedures for carrying out testing. It also covers non-standard methods, as well as those developed by the laboratory itself.

You can't do without this certification, since it is required by all organizations that perform lab testing or calibration of any kind.

ii)   State licenses for Cannabis

You will also need licenses issued by your particular state. According to the Medical Cannabis Regulation and Safety Act (MCRSA) (http://bit.ly/2TqZT1V), you are specifically required to acquire license type-8. Type-8 license covers testing of Cannabis before submission to dispensaries as well as other businesses.

iii)   Fire codes and Standards

This is to cover fire accidents. You will need to consult with your local Fire Department to find out more about this.

iv)   Quality Assurance/ Quality Control

You will need to have these programs in place so that high quality testing is assured.

v)   Standard Operating Procedures (SOPs)

These are documents that lay out the steps you will need to go through when performing certain tasks so that you remain compliant with industry standards and regulations.

Nevertheless, you should expect laws to keep changing in this industry, so you should do your best to stay current.

Step 2: Understanding the supply chain of Cannabis

After understanding the legal implications of your decision and obtaining the necessary documentation, your next step is that of analyzing the Cannabis supply chain so that you best understand what role you will be playing in each part.

Let's look briefly at some members you will be serving, and how.

i) Growers

You will be testing produce from farmers. This is to make sure that the farmers are able to guarantee that their products are free from things like mold, fungus, pesticides and other potentially harmful residues.

ii) Distributors

You will be serving distributors as well.

You will be testing the products they handle so that you can prevent false claims they may make about the specific Cannabinoid, the potency as well as DNA strain.

iii) Regulators

Regulators also depend on testing labs before they can set industry regulations, so you can be instrumental to them.

Now that you understand the role you will be playing in the industry as well as the services you will be providing, what next?

Step 3: Selecting a location and designing your lab

After going through the above steps, your next challenge is determining where you will set up your lab. The location has to comply with the laws of your state as well; you can't just set up shop anywhere. You will have to do your homework on that and negotiate with landlords.

After getting a suitable location, you will also need to ensure that the lab is designed in accordance with the laws. It should be designed in such a way that it protects you and your employees.

Areas you may want to pay special attention include:

- **Storage**: You should have proper Cannabis storage cabinets installed, as well as places to store your casework.

- **Safety**: Safety equipment like emergency showers, eyewash stations, flammable gas alarm systems and the like are requirements that you cannot do without.

- **Working areas**: Furniture of high quality such as workbenches, lab tables, carts and ventilation hoods are required.

Looking at all these requirements, don't you think it would be easier if you just worked with a partner that took care of all these details and just handed you the tab? I thought so too.

You would be happy to find that One point Solutions have been dealing with designing labs for more than a decade now and they have designed Cannabis labs and are familiar with the ins and outs of that operation. I imagine that you will be delighted to work with them. You can find them at http://bit.ly/33xLbKS

After that, you should start hiring professional staff.

Step 4: Hiring professionals

It doesn't take a genius to know that you can't run a Cannabis lab by yourself. You will need to hire professionals to help you provide the services you intend to sell.

The truth is that there isn't any specific criteria regarding hiring professionals in any field. You can create your own. But, I thought you might be interested in listening to this podcast (http://bit.ly/2yUErsz) that covers various issues regarding hiring in the Cannabis industry.

It includes the views of Kara Bradford, a consummate professional who also happens to be the CEO of Viridian Staffing, a recruiting agency for the cannabis industry.

Step 5: Procuring lab equipment

Lastly, you will need to procure top-notch equipment for conducting your lab work.

Some things you may want to keep in mind include:

- **Mass spectrometry (MC)**

These are equipment with the capacity to carry out tests to confirm presence of toxins such as pesticides and many other chemicals in Cannabis

- ***Liquid chromatography (HPLC)***

The main equipment used in determining potency levels of cannabinoids like THC, CBD, THCA and the like.

- ***Gas chromatography (GC)***

These equipment help identify Cannabinoid classifications. They help in measuring potency levels as well as well as residual solvents.

As you can see, operating a Cannabis lab is every bit as complicated as it gets. But, if you have the right constitution for it, as well as the funds, you can go for it.

#5. Start An Online Shop

The digital revolution has taken over. It's no longer necessary to run a brick and mortar store unless you really have to. And that applies to the legal Cannabis industry as well. You can open an online shop and still make sales, perhaps even do better.

Let's talk about this exciting option and how you can tap into it.

First, let me explain why it could be better.

Fewer headaches

Earlier, we talked about how finding a suitable place to set up your brick and mortar store can be quite a headache.

There are several rules by the government that ban you from setting up shop in certain areas. Furthermore, the federal government keeps pressure on landlords so that they avoid hosting potentially illegal drug dealers. Things like this only make your job of finding a suitable place to operate much harder.

Online, you do not have that problem. You can move at a much faster pace and get things done.

Cheaper

Yes, operating online is way cheaper than running a brick and mortar store.

Think of the monthly rent payments you would have to pay to your landlord. If you keep in mind that the law requires you to remit taxes before expenses for proceeds in the Marijuana business, the money you pay to your landlord is likely to take up a huge chunk of that sum.

I agree that it is far better to cut costs down in business whenever you can if you don't want to end up hurting the business. When you operate online, you get the chance to take care of that problem easily.

Freedom

In some ways, opening a physical store ties you to that very area that you have set up shop. Unless you hire someone else to run the business (very unlikely in the early stages) on your behalf, you will have to be there every day and will perhaps have to take up residence nearby.

But when you operate online, you can run your store from literally anywhere in the world. As long as you can easily contact your local supplier on the ground, you can move to whatever place you want provided you carry your computer with you and can easily access the internet.

You just receive orders and instruct your men on the ground to make a delivery. How cool is that!

Supplement offline sales

Last but not the least, you can operate both an online as well as an offline store at the same time.

If you have operated your offline dispensary and have tasted a little success and would like to diversify your operations even further, you can move on to the cyberspace. That way, you may even have some of your loyal customers thanking you since many of them may prefer shopping online and having items delivered at their home since that provides even more privacy.

It also allows you to reach other markets if you obtain legal permission to sell to those states. You can easily become one of the major Cannabis market players if you operate this way. In other words, going online is a potential game changer.

So, let's go through a number of steps you can go through before you start operating your online cannabis shop.

Step 1: Get the legal documentation.

As always, you will need to begin by considering legal matters first. At the end of the day, you will need to register a business that operates legally and sells to residents of a particular state.

So, you can seek the professional services of a lawyer in acquiring the necessary documentation that allow you to do this. They will know where to go and what to do, which can save you a lot of wasted time if you were to do things on your own.

They can also advice you on the legal boundaries you are not supposed to cross, so that you can avoid trouble.

Once you get the necessary documentation from the state you wish to operate in, you can move to step 2.

Step 2: Purchase domain and hosting

The second step involves kick-starting the process of setting up your website.

And when it comes to this step, there isn't anything different about it. You simply go through the same steps we went through when covering Cannabis blogging. If you do not remember the details, I implore you to go back and remind yourself of the things we discussed there.

I still maintain that you have to pick a name that resonates with what your business does – which in this case is dealing Cannabis products. There many reasons why you should do so. One of the most significant ones is for marketing purposes.

You see, search engines will tend to rank websites with such names higher than those with names that are out of context. So www.cannabis-shop.com may appear higher up in search results than a website that's in the same business that doesn't have a name that reflects that (for instance www.redux.com).

So, purchase your domain and hosting as per the instructions that I gave and move on to step 3.

One more thing, be sure to purchase an SSL certificate and have it installed. An SSL certificate serves two purposes. First, it identifies your website as trustworthy and this enhances the trust that people give your website. It also encrypts the information being exchanged to prevent third party onlookers from taking a peak into the data and using it maliciously. This is important for an e-commerce website that exchanges financial data.

Step 3: Select an e-commerce solution.

So you have bought your domain as well as your hosting and your hosting provider has sent you the details pertaining your website. Good, it's time to consider which e-commerce solution you are going to use.

You see, e-commerce has come a long way; most people who are not familiar with technology may not know this fact. Websites like Amazon.com and Alibaba.com may have been developed from scratch, but for you, that isn't necessary. You can set up an equally powerful e-commerce website in less than a day.

You may not get the advanced custom features those high profile websites have, but who needs them when you are just a sole proprietor who is starting out? You will get all the standard features you will need to operate an online business efficiently and that is what matters.

So how do you set up a powerful e-commerce website that fast? It's easy; simply use e-commerce software. And when it comes to that, there are plenty of them that are completely free; you won't have to pay a dime for them. The best known ones are Woocommerce, Prestashop and Magento.

My personal favorite is Woocommerce since it is developed for WordPress. You know the blogging platform we talked about earlier? All you have to do is install WordPress on your site and then install WooCommerce. The entire process is a simple point and click process. You can watch this video (http://bit.ly/2NokskD) which shows you how you can do that from start to finish.

If you aren't technically inclined, you can call in a WordPress expert who can handle the details for you. However, I can assure you that it is something you can learn and do by yourself. The beauty of working with WordPress over other platforms is that it is so popular, you can literally find a tutorial on anything that gives you trouble.

After installing WordPress plus Woocommerce, you need to move to the next step – choosing a design.

Step 4: Choose a design

You have installed the most powerful ecommerce solution on top of the most popular Content Management System ever – WordPress, so far so good.

Now you have to choose the design for your website. Again, things here are similar to our discussion of Cannabis blogging. You head over to the most popular design marketplaces on the web Themeforest and Envato.

This can be the most exciting step and yet the most troublesome. Why?

Because you will have endless options of striking designs to choose from. There are countless template (or theme) vendors in the marketplace and many of their products are well designed. However, don't get hung up on them for too long; make up your mind quickly and pick whichever theme appeals to you the most.

Again, most of them come at a friendly price. You will hardly pay more than $60 for a top-of-the-range theme. Once you get the theme, install it, or get someone to help you out. But I doubt this will be a problem since most of them are so professionally documented, you can even find additional videos documenting how to install them step by step.

Once you are done installing your design, you are good to go. Now it is time to start adding products to your website.

Step 5: Adding products to your site

IF you follow the steps in the documentation of the theme you bought, you should be staring at a beautiful shopping website hosted under your preferred domain, with demo content.

It is up to you to substitute that content with that of your own – particularly the listed products. This is where the real work is. It can take you close to a week, if not more, to photograph your products professionally and add them to your website and deleting the demo products from the site.

Remember, adding products will also include other details such as pricing information. You can compare it to stocking products in physical store – a lengthy, boring and cumbersome process.

You can allow yourself to be patient with this step, because once it is done, you will definitely feel a sense of accomplishment which makes the work feel worthwhile.

Once you are done, you can take another look at the website to determine whether you like what you see. If you do, it is time to add payment options so that you can launch the site to the public.

Step 6: Set up payment options

Setting up payment options is actually an easy process. Woocommerce is a powerful e-Commerce software for good reason, it offers you the option to add almost every payment solution that is in existence.

You can rest assured, that the most popular one – which quite frankly are what most of your customers are going to use – are fully supported, and for free.

If your theme was professionally developed and well documented, you should find instructions on how to set up payment options in the documentation that comes along with the theme. Nevertheless, there are many tutorials out there that can show you how to do that. This video http://bit.ly/2KBRwMI is my personal favorite. You can check out others as well, the solutions are everywhere.

Once you do, you can allow yourself to feel good because you have navigated the hardest part of this process. It's time to move on to step 7.

Step 7: Conduct marketing

No business can survive without marketing, and you would be wrong to assume that despite your hard work, you are all set.

Marketing is a challenging and ongoing part of your business and that is what you will have to deal with as your seventh step.

Nonetheless, as I have said many times before, marketing isn't a problem with easy and quick solutions. It is a matter that needs heavy investment in terms of time and money time after time. You may even have to bring in a professional team to help you with it.

I could write a book on marketing for online businesses, but sadly, the world doesn't need another one from me. As it is, there are countless books on the subject out there. My advice: Read as many as you can but make sure you read those written by recognized experts who are actually in the business of online marketing. There are many wannabe authors out there who are offering readers with a lot of useless recycled junk.

Step 8: Take orders and make deliveries

If you have done everything to this point, and things are working perfectly, you should start receiving orders.

Congratulations, you have now set up a real business that is working. Now, it is time for you to fulfill those orders by confirming them and making the deliveries to the destinations of choice for your customers.

Let's move on to other options.

#6. Growing Cannabis

Another viable option for you is to invest in growing Cannabis.

This makes sense because at the end of the day, the Cannabis industry will have to source products from somewhere. So participating in the creation of the key raw material in the process places you at an advantageous position.

The truth is; many people shy away from this option because they perceive growing Cannabis as a complicated process that they are not equipped to handle.

I am here to assure you that growing Cannabis can only be as hard as you make it. With just a little bit of knowledge – which I provide in this section – all of a sudden, growing Cannabis isn't that hard. If you have ever learnt anything, then u can handle it.

As you go through the step-by-step process I lay out for you, you will realize that your fear of the practice was completely unfounded.

In fact, as you will soon find out, once you get the hang of it, growing Cannabis isn't as hard as other economic activities in the Cannabis industry.

So, are you ready to try your hand at growing Cannabis? Great. Let's get started.

Step 1: Figure out the legality of growing Cannabis

At this point, this should be a no-brainer.

After going through this step over and over in nearly every economic activity we have described in this book, if you go ahead and cultivate marijuana without finding out whether it is legal to do so, or even obtaining the legal paperwork, you will only have yourself to blame.

That said, let's not spend any more time on this than we need to. Let's move on to the next step.

Step 2: Choose your favorite strain

Your next step after determining the legality of marijuana and obtaining the necessary paperwork is to choose the strain that you will grow.

You need to do this before everything else because, different Cannabis strains are meant for different purposes. So, at the very least, you need to determine your why before you go into the how.

A few useful questions to ask yourself at this point would be:

- What is my primary motivation for growing this Cannabis?

- Am I growing this for the recreational market or the medical market?

- Who is my target market? What do they specialize in? Is this the right strain for them?

- What is my timeline for getting my product to the market?

Questions like these may help you determine the best strain you need to choose.

To make you better understand why you need to make choices like these, let us look at the three main Cannabis categories along with their properties

i) *Cannabis sativa strains*

- Promote an easy and lively effect
- Best if you want to induce psychedelic effects
- Mainly used for recreational purposes
- Have a tendency to grow tall especially during flowering phase
- Can be heat-resistant
- They tend to develop long buds

ii) *Cannabis indica strains*

- Promote heavy and relaxing effects
- Best for sedative or sleeping effects
- Mainly used for recreational purposes
- Have a short appearance
- Can tolerate cool conditions
- Tend to develop dense buds

iii) *Auto-flowering strains (a blend of sativa and indica strains)*

- Best for medical use
- Can also be used for mild recreational purposes
- Are small in size
- Have a short cycle of 2 to 3 months
- Ideal for beginning farmers

I can't decide for you, but I am guessing that after looking at these properties, you are now more informed on the direction you need to take.

Let's move on.

Step 3: Prepare the space to grow

The next thing to do is to consider the place where your Cannabis will be grown.

Remember, when it comes to cultivating Cannabis, you have the option of growing them outside or indoors. Growing Cannabis indoors offers you the most control over the environmental factors that affect the growth. So, it is always the best option for commercial cultivation of Cannabis.

You have prepare the space that you will grow Cannabis the right way. And when it comes this, there are specific rules to follow. Let us look at what they are:

Rule 1: Lighting

The first rule has to do with lighting. As with any other plant, Cannabis plants need light for photosynthesis as well.

However, if you grow the plant indoors, then you will need to provide artificial lighting that you can control. Therefore, you will need to make sure that your room is completely light proof. This allows you to control the hours of lighting and the hours of darkness.

There are many types of lighting bulbs out there that you could use, but **LED grow lights** are by far the best. They last longer, consume less energy and are well designed to suit the purpose. Place one for every square meter.

Also, make sure the room is reflective so that you can optimally make use of the light. Paint the walls white to ensure this.

Rule 2: Air circulation and ventilation

Get a room that is air-tight but one that also has vents fitted with carbon filters so that the air that gets out is cleaned to avoid disturbing nearby residents with Cannabis smell.

Put fans as well in the premises to ensure that air circulation is consistent. An air extractor also needs to be present so that it can get the odor off the plants and regulate the temperatures inside the room. Ideally, temperature should range between 64ºF and 86ºF.

Rule 3: Water

Inevitably, water will run down to the floor when you water the plants. Because of this, you will need to have a waterproof floor that lets the water out of the premises.

You will also need to control the humidity inside the room because too much of it can lead to growth of fungi and molds. So make sure you have a dehumidifier in place.

Rule 4: Nutrients

You will need to provide nutrients to your plants so that they can grow to be healthy and productive. We will cover them later on, but for now, realize that you will need to have them in place as part of your preparation.

After preparing as advised, you should move to the next step.

Step 4: Propagate the Cannabis

Your next step involves actually growing the Cannabis plants themselves. This is the part you have been waiting for.

So how do you go about it?

I'll show you how.

So the first thing that you need to understand is that there are two methods of propagating Cannabis: cloning and planting seeds.

The cloning option sounds a little bit more interesting so we will start with it.

Cloning a Cannabis plant

The cloning option is by far the best way of creating new Cannabis plants. It is also the most popular method, and for good reason.

So what is cloning anyway?

Cloning (at least as it applies to plants) is simply the practice of growing new plants from parts of an existing one. In this case, you will be growing new Cannabis plants from cuttings of an existing one. Another word for cloning is vegetative propagation.

The cutting you make from the original plant develops roots of its own and grows into a plant.

But why does cloning work?

It's quite simple. Cloning works because parts of plants are made from undifferentiated cells. These cells (otherwise known as meristem cells) have the capability of growing into other parts of the plant such as roots, leaves, flowers, and so on. Once they develop, the cutting becomes another plant.

Okay, so now you know why cloning works, so why is it so popular?

Cloning is popular because it is the best method of ensuring you produce plants with the same desirable features like that you may have observed. This means that you can produce a plant with the same flowering characteristics, temperature tolerance, gender, and other characteristics.

The gender aspect is especially important since, in the Cannabis industry, this matters a lot. You see, female plants hold the most value because they are the ones capable of producing buds, which are then harvested for commercial purposes.

This isn't the case with male plants. They produce pollen sacs, which don't contain the cannabinoids. In fact, you need to watch out for them. If you happen to spot one in the middle of a commercial project, you need to remove it as it may pollinate the females and the buds then develop into seeds.

The only useful purpose that the male Cannabis plants serve is to help with breeding, through facilitating the production of seeds. Otherwise, they hold little commercial value.

So how do you do it – clone a Cannabis plant?

It's pretty easy simple. We are going to look at an example of how you do this for just one plant. Then, it will be up to you to replicate the process on a commercial scale.

Just do the following:

i) First, get a sharp razor blade or a pair of scissors, rooting hormone, a glass container that has growing medium (for instance coconut fiber) and a spray bottle with water in it.

ii) Second, water your growing medium. The idea is to keep the medium moist, not wet. So make sure you do not pour excess water on it.

iii) Next, choose the pant that has the traits that impress you the most; since you will be creating an exact replica of that plant.

iv) Ensure that the plant you select has been watered. Ideally, you want the plant to have been be watered for around 3 days before you start cutting off parts of it. The reason for this measure is so that you ensure that the plant has washed down the nitrogen. This makes it easier for the cutting to develop roots.

v) Also make sure that you have washed your hands and have sterilized your hands because cuttings are always delicate.

vi) Select a growing tip of the plant. Select one that preferably has at least two leaf internodes and is at least 3 to 6 inches in length.

vii) Make the cutting using either a sterilized blade or pair of scissors (or anything that works really). Make sure you make the incision at a 45° angle.

viii) Apply rooting hormone onto the cut surface of the tip and then carefully place the cutting in the growing medium. Be gentle, taking care not to apply too much pressure as you force the cutting into the medium. Then, spray water onto the cutting, but not too much.

From now on, your job is to make sure that the plant and the medium stay moist. Remember, the goal is not to keep them wet, as this might facilitate growth of fungi.

Also, allow the cutting to access daylight. You can take it out. Or you can place it under LED light.

After a week or so, the cutting should start developing some roots. If you look at the plant and verify that it looks stable and healthy, you can move it to into soil.

IF everything goes according to plan, you should have no problem. Congratulations you have just successfully cloned a Cannabis plant for the first time.

But what about propagation through seeds? Let us look at that as well.

Propagation Cannabis through seeds

The good thing with propagating through seeds is that it is nothing complicated. Chances are, if you have ever planted a seed in your life, you are already familiar with the process.

Nevertheless, let us look at what it entails.

i) First of all, make sure you have a medium that is sterile. The point of this is so that you can ensure there will be no growth of fungi.

ii) Also, make sure that the medium is deep enough to allow for the free development of roots.

iii) The next thing you do is soak the seeds in water. Keep them there for around 2 to 3 hours before planting them in the medium.

iv) Next, spray some water over the medium to keep it moist. But, take care not to make it wet.

v) Also, make sure some light as well as air can penetrate the medium.

From this point onwards, your job is to wait. Most seedlings germinate after five days. You should expect the same. After the germination of the seedling, you can start applying fertilizer onto the medium.

That's it concerning the propagation of Cannabis plants. Moving on, we look at how you can provide care to your plants in the vegetative stage

Step 4: Caring for plants in vegetative stage

The vegetative stage of a plant is the period of growth that follows germination, and lasts all the way to the flowering stage.

This is a critical stage for your Cannabis plants and you will need the know-how of taking care of them.

So, what do you do?

The first thing you will need to take care of is the lighting. The plants will need more lighting at this stage because, it is necessary for photosynthesis, which also leads to growth.

As a rule, your plants will need access to lighting for at least 18 hours. This means that your growth LED lamps will need to stay on for that amount of time.

The next thing you do is apply the right nutrient mix. It is recommended that you provide your plants with a high amount of Nitrogen, a medium amount of Phosphorous, and a low amount of Potassium.

The good thing is that there are fertilizers on sale in the market that have been prepared with the vegetative stage of Cannabis plants in mind. You just have to apply them as they are. The best known one is Dyna-Gro.

Dyna-Gro is a fertilizer that can be applied to any medium be it soil, water, or a soilless mix. This makes it your best choice in this business.

It comes in two varieties: **Grow** and **Bloom**. The Grow flavor is meant for applying to plants in the vegetative stage. It contains the right composition of all the nutrients needed. Afterwards, when your plants move into the flowering or budding stage, you are required to apply the Bloom flavor.

As for the instructions on how you can apply the fertilizers, you can find them well laid out on a sticker placed on the bottle. They are all pretty easy to follow.

There is also the question of what kind of water you are supposed to use in growing Cannabis. This is a fair question to ask. Generally, regular tap water is fine as long as it's "hardness" isn't too much. Hardness is measured in parts per million (or PPM in short). If you test the hardness and find that it ranges anywhere between 200 and 300 PPM, you can be assured that it is safe.

However, if the level of harness is higher than that, then it's probably not safe to use it. You can opt to use Reverse Osmosis to refine the water and lower the hardness. However, you will need to add Cal-mag so that you can account for lost minerals and nutrients that are naturally found in water due to the process.

One last thing: you also need to ensure that the pH around the roots is at the optimum level. pH is important because it assists in the uptake of nutrients by the roots of the plant. If it is too high or too low, you will have problems. Ideally, your pH should range between 6.0 to 7.0 for a soil medium and 5.5 to 6.5 for a hydroponics medium.

Fortunately for you, there are pH-testing kits that let you carry out tests on your own. Also, there are chemicals that you can apply to the medium so that you can raise or lower the pH accordingly.

Make sure that in the course of your project, you test the pH so that you can adjust it accordingly.

Step 5: Caring for the plants in the flowering stage

You know that your plants have entered the flowering stage once you start spotting buds. This stage lasts all the way to harvesting, which is about 8 weeks.

Special care is needed here as well, so how do you provide it?

The first thing you will need to change is the amount of time that you provide the lighting. It is generally recommended that you provide 12 hours of lighting. This means that you will also have to leave the plants in 12 hours of darkness.

The nutrient requirements also change at this point. This is because unlike during the vegetative stage, at this stage, the growth has slowed down. Therefore, you will have to apply the Bloom flavor of the Dyna-gro fertilizer as I indicated earlier. It will take care of the nutrient requirements of the plant.

Another thing you will need to do is remove/uproot any male plants that may exist in the facility.

How do you tell the two apart?

It's easy. The male ones have growing balls, which are really pollen sacs. The female ones have white hairs, which are really the pistils. These pistils later grow into the buds. You want to avoid pollination so the male plants need to be taken out of the facility.

Also, humidity will need to be maintained at 45%. Get a thermos-hygrometer and a de-humidifier on site to help you regulate humidity levels accordingly. This is because excess humidity poses the risk of encouraging growth of fungi and/or mold.

In addition to the above, make sure you provide support for buds that become heavy so that they get access to light. Also trim excess leaves so that light can penetrate well. It also makes sure that the plant dedicates its resources to growth of buds. Dry leaves and branches should be removed as well. But take care not cut more leaves than you need to; otherwise, you run the risk of jeopardizing the plant's health.

It is vital that you pay extra attention to you plants at this stage since this is the time when your plants are most vulnerable. It is also the stage that is directly responsible for the result you get out of the entire project. A few things going wrong at this stage can seriously hamper your productivity.

Step 6: Harvesting

You know you have entered the harvesting period when you start noticing that no new white hairs (or pistils) are forming. When you see that, start preparing for harvesting.

A crucial aspect of harvesting is that timing is key. If you harvest too early, you risk ending up with low potency buds. If you wait too long, you may find that the amount of THC in the buds has dropped to critical levels. So, you will need to be hard on the details of timing.

So, when is the right time to harvest the buds?

You harvest when you notice that around 50% to 70% of the white hairs have darkened.

The harvesting process involves cutting down the plant, and trimming the excess leaves all the way to the bud, taking care not to be sloppy. You should end up with buds alone as shown in the picture below.

After that, your next job is to **let the buds dry**. To do this, simply hang them upside down and leave them in an environment with good air circulation and less than 45% humidity. The temperature should also be at around 70 degrees, but in a dark room. The amount of time it takes them to dry is at least 7 days.

After they dry up, you should notice that they have lost about 75% of their original weight. That's perfectly fine. Now it's time to go through a process known as **curing**.

To cure the buds, place them in jars to around ¾ full. Tightly close the jars and place them in a cool dark place. Open the jars on a daily basis for a few minutes so that moisture is dispelled and fresh air gets in. Do this for up to 3 weeks. You may want to extend the curing period but do not go beyond 6 weeks because from then on, nothing changes about the buds.

That's all there is to it. From then on, you can deliver them to a lab for testing or do with them as you wish.

Lastly, let us cover another investment opportunity that is open to all – buying stock in Cannabis companies.

#7. Buying Stock In Cannabis Companies

If you come from a state that hasn't legalized Cannabis yet, you have probably been reading this book thinking that you have been cut off from this wonderful investment opportunity. I assure you that is not the case. There is an opportunity for everyone in this industry. And this opportunity doesn't come with the excess baggage of doing all the dirty work. That opportunity is Cannabis stocks.

Yes, as long as you can afford some money, you can put it in a company that operates in the Cannabis industry and get a share of its profits. And this isn't an opportunity for bottom-feeders only by the way. This morning, August 2nd 2019, I woke up to the news that Aphria stock had just jumped 38% after a surprise profits announcement: https://on.mktw.net/2KKqcMl

If you had invested in such a stock, you would be smiling right now. But it isn't too late. You can fully expect similar events to occur in the future. And that is why I have gone through the trouble of providing you with a detailed guide of how you can invest in Cannabis stocks.

Investing in stocks is a wide topic that could easily take up a book of its own. However, in this guide, I will be looking to get straight to the point in the most efficient way possible.

I have tried to distil the information down to just a few steps that anyone can easily follow and get a good result from their investment. I have also tried to keep in mind that you may have little to no experience investing in the stock market, so I resort to explaining the basics without going too deep into unnecessary details.

Without wasting any more time, let's get down to business.

Step 1: Choosing a good broker

Your journey to investing in Cannabis stocks begins with selecting a good broker.

But who is a broker?

Put simply, a broker is a person or an entity whose job is to execute financial transactions in the stock and other financial markets, on behalf of clients. The clients of a broker can be ordinary individuals like you and I, or it can be companies and huge corporations. A broker usually receives a commission in their line of work.

Legal Cannabis Will Be Bigger Than Cryptos

The important thing to understand is that brokers sit midway between you and the stock market and because of this role, they are at times given the name **market makers**.

The quality of your investment is in some ways related to the kind of broker you choose. So, you want to select the best broker you can possibly get. And when it comes to this, there are things that you need to look out for. Let's look at some of them.

1) Security

Security is the first thing you look for in this process.

After all, you will be trusting your broker to handle your money for you. You need to know that you can trust them.

So, first of all, make sure that your broker is regulated by the relevant government body in the country it operates in. In the U.S, that would be the Securities and Exchange Commission (SEC). Your broker should have no problem providing you with proof of this. As a matter of fact, they usually include it in the official website.

Also, you need to check the quality of the website. How is the design? Does it look professional? A poor design is a dead giveaway of the quality of work that went into that website. And that provides insights into the security of the site as well.

Also be sure that the address of the site begins with https://www instead of just http://www. The first one shows that the site information is encrypted from third party onlookers in transit while the second one isn't. This is important for a site that exchanges financial data.

If everything checks out, then you should look at the next important thing

2) Transaction costs

Your broker makes most of their money from commissions. You want to make sure that these costs are as low as possible; otherwise, they could eat into your financial gains.

The only way to verify this information is to ask for the information from the broker and comparing it with that of other brokers in the business. If the difference is reasonable, then you can go ahead.

One thing though: don't select a broker based on such criteria alone. You may find a bad broker using low transaction costs to mask his incompetence.

3) Deposits and withdrawals

Your broker should also make it easy for you to deposit to and withdraw money from your account.

Usually, this is information that you can always get by performing a simple Google search. Chances are, if your broker has a problem with this, people are aware of it and have discussed it on forums on the internet. If you find that this is the case, then you can either check with the company or cross that broker off your list.

4) Customer service

Your broker should also provide great customer service. He or she should be available for 24 hours round the clock.

Check to see that they have a live chat support on their website. Also check to see if it works. For most of the queries you may have about the company, you can submit them here to verify that the support works.

In my experience, I have never found this to be a problem with a broker who has gone to great lengths to show that they are trustworthy.

If you would like some suggestions of some good brokers, you can try any one on this list:

- TD Ameritrade
- Fidelity Investments
- Charles Schwab
- Interactive brokers
- Trade Station

Step 2: Opening a brokerage account

After you have pinpointed your broker of choice, you will need to open an account with them.

A brokerage account is similar to a bank account. The only difference is that it is meant to hold your investment funds in a particular market.

The process is usually easy and self-explanatory, especially if you are working with a reputable broker. They may ask for scanned copies of identity and proof of residence after which the account creation and verification process should be successful.

Step 3: Depositing your money into the account

The next step is to deposit money into your brokerage account.

This is always is easy. You just move funds from your bank account to the brokerage account. Your broker will provide you with a variety of means to this. You could use a credit card, a wired transfer, PayPal or some other means that you prefer.

After the money has been deposited and reflected on your account, you should move to the next step.

Step 4: Selecting the company to invest in

Of all the steps in the process of investing, this is the most important one. This step is what ultimately determines whether you will succeed or not. If the company you purchase stock in performs poorly in the period following your order, you lose money and your investment may be rendered worthless.

So, how do you determine what company to invest in?

Unfortunately the answer to that question is never easy. People have looked into that matter for decades ever since the concept of the stock market came to light. Countless strategies have been developed to help guide this process.

Some are good, some aren't.

Nevertheless, I will provide you with a method of selection that has stood the test of time. In fact, it has been so successful, the world's most successful investor (Warren Buffet) credits his extraordinary success to it.

That method is called **value investing**. It is ideal for this purpose since I assume that you will be looking to invest for the long-term. The good thing about it is that it helps you invest in undervalued companies that can perform well once the industry sentiment kicks in. It also helps you eliminate high risk companies that may end up destroying your portfolio.

It is my favorite method and I will show you how you can use it to select stocks that can end up being major winners in the near future.

Let's begin.

i) *Quality rating*

The first criteria you use to pinpoint the right stock is the quality of the stock.

This makes sense because whatever you do, you do not want to invest in a company that has a poor rating.

Stocks are valued based on their ability to pay back money that they owe, or in other words, credit. If a stock has demonstrated a high ability to pay back its creditors, it is given a high rating. If it is incapable of paying its creditors, the rating is lowered.

This is a good merit because if the company that you invest in fails to pay back its debts, it may soon become insolvent.

So what rating should you be looking for in this regard?

Benjamin Graham, the man behind this strategy, recommends that you use Standard and Poor's (S&P's) rating system. Select a **rating of B or higher**. Anything below B is unacceptable.

ii) *Debt to current asset ratio*

The next metric that you should pay attention to is the debt to current asset ratio.

This is a ratio that looks into the debt of a company, relative to the amount of assets that it owns. In other words, it looks at how many assets of the company have been leveraged to acquire financing.

A good idea in value investing is to go for companies that have a debt load that isn't dangerously high. If the ratio is high, it follows then that the debt load to the company is high and vice versa.

It is recommended that as an investor, you pick a company that has a debt to current asset ratio that is either 1.10 or less. A company with a ratio higher than that should be disregarded.

You can find data on Debt to Current Asset ratios with Standard and Poor's as well.

iii) Current ratio

The Current Ratio is another important thing to look into.

But what is it and what does it imply?

The current ratio is a measure of the assets of a company against its liabilities. The importance of this metric is to communicate to investors how capable the company is in meeting its short-term debt obligations (those within a year).

Your concern is to select a stock that has this ratio at nothing less than 1.50. Once again, this number can be provided by Standard and Poor's. A qualified accountant can help you come up with this number as well.

iv) Earnings per share growth (EPS)

You should also be able to spot a positive earnings per share growth across the years.

But what is earnings per share?

It's a number determined by dividing the profit of a company by the outstanding shares. EPS growth shows how that number has grown over a 12-month period, expressed as a percentage. It depicts growth in profitability.

You should be able to see a positive growth for at least 5 years. However, since the Cannabis industry has been around for a short while, you can reduce that range.

v) Price to earnings per share ratio

This metric looks at the price of a company's stock against the EPS. It is also a way to gauge performance of the company over time.

Take companies that have a number that is 9.0 or less. This gets rid of companies that have grown too fast. Remember, you want to catch the wave before it starts not midway or close to the end. So this is very important.

vi) Price to book value (P/BV)

This ratio looks at the market value of a stock relative to its book value.

You see, the financial markets are never efficient. Companies frequently trade at prices that are not a reflection of their true value. A price to book value ratio helps you to establish this fact.

It is a far better alternative to the P/E ratios which are deemed misleading at times. It is meant to show whether a company is overvalued or undervalued.

As a rule, select companies with a price to book value that is less than 1.20. This is because you want to buy a company whose price is either close to or below its market value.

vii) Dividends

Lastly, make sure you invest in a company that pays a dividend.

This ensures that you get some return on your investment as you wait for the market to make up its mind on moving the stock - which could take a considerable amount of time.

Take a look at the companies that fit the criteria above and select those companies as good candidates for your investment.

Top companies to keep under your radar

It would be better if I provided you with a list of reputable companies in the Cannabis industry that have shown a lot of promise and that should definitely be under your radar.

I am not recommending that you buy these stocks right off the bat. No, that would be unwise. I am just stating that you should look into them. You can use a value investing approach or some other strategy of your own. If your analysis shows you that they are a good bet, you should take them.

Those companies are:

- Canopy Growth Corp (CGC)
- Tilray (TLRY)
- Aurora Cannabis (ACB)
- Cronos Group (CRON)
- Aphria (APHA)
- Constellation Brands (STZ)
- Alcanna Inc. (CLIQ)
- Botanix Pharmaceuticals Limited (BOT)
- Organigram Holding Inc. (OGI)

- Valens Groworks Corp (VGW)
- MedmenEnterprises Inc, (MMEN)

Next, look into how much you will invest.

Step 6: Determine how much you will invest

After picking the ideal targets for your investment, your next task is to decide how much you will invest in the companies.

Most of the time, this is a personal matter. Only you can determine how comfortable you are with a certain company and allocate your money accordingly.

When is doubt, just divide your investment capital equally across the companies.

One thing to keep in mind is that you should never put all your money in one company. You should diversify at least. Even though value investing is one of the most powerful strategies available, it is not foolproof. Nothing in the investment world ever is. Anything can go wrong and the company goes under. Diversifying reduces you're your overall portfolio risk.

Step 7: Placing your order

After determining how much to put in each company, you should have no problem making your investment.

This is where you go ahead and place your order with your broker.

Legal Cannabis Will Be Bigger Than Cryptos

The way you do this is through some trading software you are provided by your broker. The moment you open an account with your broker, you are always provided with a link to download a piece of software that helps you access the stock market and monitor prices. This software also allows you to place orders to buy stocks or sell them, along with other features.

You simply look for the ticker symbol of the company you want to invest in and click to it. You then determine the size of the position and click buy and sell.

Now you need to understand that position sizing may require you to perform mathematical calculations. It is simply a way of determining how much money you will stake on a company.

I have encountered trading platforms that handle this for you. You simply enter the amount you are willing to invest and the software takes care of the rest. So this depends on the trading software your broker issues you.

But, if you are having problems with this, you can speak to your broker. They are always happy to assist customers with matters like these as part of their customer service.

Another thing to remember is that you will be using market orders. Be sure to communicate that with your broker as you ask for assistance. Other orders like limit orders are meant for speculators, who are another class of investors entirely. This book won't be going into stock speculation strategies but there are other books out there you could consult.

Step 8: Keeping an eye on your investment

Your last step is to monitor your investment.

There are many ways to do this. You can watch the news to find out what is happening out there. You can also check on periodic reports sent to you by the company by the way of email.

The idea is to check and see that the company's financials are healthy and the management is solid. This is something that you will always do from time – maybe for years – for as long as you are invested in the company.

CONCLUSION

We have finally come to the concluding part of this book.

I want to thank you for your attention and your support throughout this book. I also want to thank you for your support in our efforts by purchasing this book once again.

It is my sincere hope that you have received the value you expected to get from this book. Investing for financial stability and prosperity is a noble pursuit and you have demonstrated your willingness to go after it by buying this book.

What I urge you is that you put whatever you have picked from this book into practice. Knowledge isn't power until it is applied.

All in all, I wish you the best of luck in your new investment projects.

If you found the book valuable, can you recommend it to others? One way to do that is to post a review on Amazon.

Thank you and good luck!

www.ingramcontent.com/pod-product-compliance
Lightning Source LLC
Chambersburg PA
CBHW070649220526
45466CB00001B/362